POETRY LONDON/APPLE MAGAZINE

Editor: Tambimuttu

'All things come back to their roots'—Lao Tzu

Cover by John Piper

Back cover color-poem by Patrick Hayman

Tailpieces by Josef Herman

Robin Williamson was recorded by John Whiting of October Sound.

David Jones' painted inscription *Kathleen* is reproduced by permission of Anthony d'Offay Gallery.

Iris Murdoch's poems reprinted by permission of the *Boston University Journal*.

John Cooper-Clarke poem courtesy of Spilt Beans.

Photography by:

Joanna Voight (Christopher Logue photo)

Keystone Press Agency (Iris Murdoch photo)

Cine Ciao (Theater of All Possibilities photo)

We are deeply appreciative of the support of the Greater London Arts Association and the kind assistance of the many friends who made this magazine possible: John and Myfanwy Piper, Lawrence Durrell, Mary Colmore, Robin Waterfield, Alan Smith, Jonathan Barker, and John and Caitlin Matthews. Special thanks to Harvey and Hugh Brendon for their loyal and steadfast assistance over many years.

POETRY LONDON/APPLE MAGAZINE

24 Old Gloucester Street, Queens Square, London WC1.
5 Beekman Street, NYC.

Editor: Tambimuttu

Associate Editors:
Jane Williams, Myfanwy Piper, Kathelin Hoffman
Harry Smith (U.S.)

Managing Editor:
Kathleen Arden Brown

Unsolicited MSS. will not be returned unless accompanied by stamped addressed envelope. The editors do not take responsibility for the loss of MSS.

ISBN 85629056 4 paperback

Printed in Great Britain by A. Wheaton & Co. Ltd., Exeter

£4.95

Lawrence Durrell

FROM THE ELEPHANT'S BACK

(Text amended and slightly expanded of a lecture first given in French at the Centre Pompidou, Paris, April 1, 1981.)

This is the first time that I have ventured to accept an invitation to lecture in France, in French, and I am happy that it should be here in Paris, at the Centre Pompidou. It is a suitable place to discuss the theory and the practice of fiction in relation to myself, and moreover in a language which prides itself on being able to make fine distinctions.

The invitation reached me at a suitable moment also, for I was between two instalments of a new constellation of novels, and pondering on its form; I thought that the act of turning my notions into French might help me to realise them more clearly and thus help me to explain, if not to excuse, the direction taken by my writing. I have nothing very esoteric to propound, no views about the novel which would justify an excursion into such disciplines as are offered by the newest sciences, like linguistics, for example. That would be too sophisticated. At the worst I might confess to using my Freud as a compass, for psychoanalysis has brought us real treasures of observation and insight which we should not neglect. Of course it does not go far enough, but then nothing does!

I would prefer to present my case in terms of biography, for my thinking is coloured by the fact that I am a colonial, an Anglo-Indian, born into that strange world of which the only great poem is the novel *Kim* by Kipling. I was brought up in its shadow, and like its author I was sent to England to be educated. The juxtaposition of the two types of consciousness was extraordinary and created, I think, an ambivalence of vision which was to both help and hinder me as a writer. At times I felt more Asiatic than European, at times the opposite; at times I felt like a white negro thinking in pidgin!

At first one hatches books, stories, poems, as they arrive, with pleasure and surprise, and quite without guarantees, as one produces babies. It is only after five or ten years that one starts to recognise a family resemblance—the blue eye, the characteristic nose—which give a specific character to the whole. One begins to trace an inner coherence which relates all these separate parts into a system of ideas or a philosophy of life of a distinctive kind. In this way your author grows his unique personality and assumes himself, just as a child does. In my case India was just as important to me as England was. I reacted creatively to both styles of vision, and I often criticised both tartly, perhaps unjustly even, for it was difficult to match such opposing attributes and to make something coherent of the lessons they taught me. One part of me has remained a child of the jungle, ever mindful of the various small initiations which an Indian childhood imposes. I have seen the Rope Trick when I was ten, and distinctly felt the hypnotic power of the conjuror over us as we sat round him in a circle. I have been followed from tree-top to tree-top by sportive monkeys which pelted me with nuts and stones. Their anger made them very accurate and I was glad I wore the stout pith helmet of my father, made of cork about two inches thick—better than a modern crash-helmet! I have seen a cobra fight a mongoose. I have seen the peak of Everest from the foot of my bed in a gaunt dormitory in Darjeeling! My first language was Hindi. And so on!

My family came to India before the great Indian Mutiny, so that neither my father nor my mother had seen England or experienced the English at home. We were virgin. My father was an engineer at an epoch when we were building the great railway system which now secures the postal system and is a life-line which helps in cases of famine or flood. The family ramified throughout India, in the police, the military, the functionaries, the technocrats. But we were real Anglo-Indians, we spoke the languages of the places, and one of my uncles and a cousin became known as translators of Buddhist texts. But what of my elephant?

One of my uncles was a district Commissioner in Bihar, that is to say a sort of Prefect in charge of a land area as large as two or three French departments. He had many duties including that of shooting elephants when, as often happened then, they went mad and attacked villages. Also tigers and rhinoceros. But the elephants caused him the most regret. My father wished me to learn to shoot and sent me to visit him—he lived in a strange sinister rambling house in Ranchi, with a large garden full of animals. I arrived at dusk to find it empty—everyone was away on a picnic. I walked round this empty house with interest for I had heard stories of this great hunter among my uncles. But I had not been prepared for the dozen or so skulls of fully grown elephants which lined the back verandah. They were huge and grave, like a Greek chorus. Why had he put them there?

During the week, when I went on my first shoot with him, I was able to interrogate him. He said that he thought that the mad elephants developed a sort of brain tumour, and that when he shot one he had the head cut off and examined. Then the sun bleached away the flesh and you were left with this big beautiful skull. I was struck by the word 'beautiful'. He said it twice. But this was not all. One of the shot elephants had left a small child behind, and this was to become my playmate during my stay. It was called Sadu. It was an apprentice elephant learning its duties with a couple of trained grown-up females. But as yet it was not very big or strong; so it took me to practice upon. It had learned to say *salaam*, to pick up money from the ground, and was now learning how to hoist a man on to its back. A grown man would have been too heavy, so Sadu was told to practise with me. This he did with pleasure. They hold out their trunks curled up at the end like a human hand; you put your foot into it and presto you are raised in the air, and placed securely on the animal's back, between those two fantastic ears, the signs of supernormal spirituality, they say. They have a singular floating walk, a little humorous, like a drunken Irishman; elephants are great comics. But the proverb says that whoever sees the world from the back of an elephant learns the secrets of the jungle and becomes a seer. I had to be content to become a poet, but it was enough for one life.

I am often asked if I was not marked by India. Obviously to live in a country where the whole population both civil and ecclesiastical was trying implacably to seek a fulcrum of repose at the heart of reality: a country where people were living alongside nature and not in tangence to it, gives off a very powerful flavour, permeating the air. On the other hand, what I was learning at school taught me that one should not become too resigned to the behaviour of nature. Famines and floods and epidemics should and could be resisted by science. So that our lives ran counter to the life of passivity which was the Indian way. Who is right? Even now the problem dogs India—can one expect to have pure drinking water and modern clinics without losing the Mantras? We were too cocksure about the matter, and gloried in the perfections of Victorian science. I remember a great savant announcing that all the secrets of the universe had been discovered and that only a few insignificant details remained to be worked out! By the time I was sixteen the whole of this scientific edifice had been undermined and was ready to crash down in ruins. Strange that there is no word for the Greek 'hubris' in English or French.

I went to school at Darjeeling with the Jesuits, though we were given a strictly secular and not religious instruction. We were about forty Protestants, Taoists, Indians, and so on. So I can say I was brought up by Jesuits, though only as an out-patient so to speak! They were very fine men, preaching by example alone, and they were impressive as indeed their religion is. But what a paradox these black figures presented in the purity of such landscapes, in the purity of these huge clouds sailing everywhere like humble space-ships. Christian prayers in all that smiling silence where the lamas walked—always secure and serene—upon the high road outside the school. It was the main road from Tibet to the plains and they passed all the time—heading for the two great Indian religious universities in the plains. Often in my dreams I hear the squeak of their little prayer wheels—a scientific device of great cunning, worthy rather of mechanists who believed that prayers can be said by a computer—another unresolved problem of our age! In America people will soon be born from computers, some people believe, while newly-invented prayer wheels work off a torch-battery and save energy for better things. Does a prayer wheel know that it is performing an act of merit in revolving? One wonders.

But meanwhile I had said goodbye to my elephant Sadu and my father had obtained a new job in the hills. It was to maintain a small mountain railway, the one that runs in the most precipitous fashion, sometimes upon gradients of one in three, up the rampart of Himalayan foothills until it arrives at Darjeeling, the terminus; after which, mules and horses carry the traveller onwards into Tibet. My father was a true Victorian and his attitude to science was, in the anthropological sense, religious. Moreover he had inherited some ten new little elephants made of steel which he adored. They were sturdy and very beautiful as you will see, and marvellous workers. They were in fact the logical positivist's version of Sadu. They really merited our adoration, and the first time we wound up the cliff-faces of the mountains we realised that they were not toys but as massively powerful as tug-boats. They had no names, but I called them all Sadu. This little locomotive was so simple! It was a *cocotte-minute*, a pressure-cooker on wheels. How had nobody thought of it before? The track ran through landscapes of dreams—just as the abandoned railway lines of the Gard along which I walk and reflect also do. Except that you had the snows and the mists always opening and closing upon sheer precipices. It was an uncanny world of strangely conflicting emanations in feeling, thought, atmosphere. You smelt Tibet!

It was of course a dramatic wrench to leave India, but I was optimistic and eager to see this marvellous distant paradise upon which we had all depended morally for so long. It was known as 'Home' which was very touching. I knew that it was better than heaven, because I had been told that everything British was better than everything foreign. I felt as pleased as a Jew, belonging to the chosen race, and I was eager to affront the problems with good grace. Luckily too my school, after a year in London, was a most beautiful public school, in Canterbury, whose architecture and atmosphere resembled very closely the school I had quitted in Darjeeling.

I gave no great trouble though I was rather neurotic and so a bad student; but I played games well and boxed so that my life was not rendered miserable like that of weaker boys. I made good friends, and the masters, like the Jesuits, were honest and lively and most competent. My French master for example on learning that I wanted to learn French and become a writer immediately took a subscription to *Le Monde* for me—the weekly literary pages. So every week I had this foreign paper. This kindly and delightful man was mad about France and French literature and encouraged my interest. His name was Mr. Hollingsworth—I found it the other day among my papers. I believe he is still alive. It's a pleasure to thank him publicly in French for he taught me my first words of the language.

But yes, it was a grave wrench leaving Sadu.

There were compensations, the most important being the language and literature, which now became my passport and in which I performed my apprentice duties. My father hoped I would become a senior functionary and return to India, no longer a petit bourgeois but a great man with an expensive dinner jacket! I was not against the idea, but I said I wished to be a writer. He said it was okay but that I must go to Oxford first. His view was that all writers should go to Oxford where they made very influential friends who helped them to become successful afterwards. Perhaps this was not so silly as it then seemed. But he had read in the paper that Bernard Shaw had three Rolls-Royces and Kipling two—he wanted me to enjoy this sort of success; but I wanted a typewriter and if such a thing had been possible, an elephant.

I got the typewriter for Christmas and a complete Shakespeare. My father was a real gentleman in the basic sense and I regret he has not lived to read the fan-mail my books have brought me over the years.

I started to write like everyone else, without having anything special to say. I never thought of my work as particularly original—it was a tesselation of other men's ideas filtered through my vision. But when I began to learn my job I knew that I was part of a splendid tradition and I hoped to do as well as my forerunners. But as I came to read them I realised just how stable their Victorian world had been and how unstable mine had become, how precarious and unsettling the new metaphysics was. What a gap stretched between Robinson Crusoe—the last novel of human isolation without loss of identity, without alienation, and Kafka's Castle in which the new sensibility had been mercilessly exposed to view. The new departures in scientific thought had unsettled and indeed had even ruptured both syntax and serial order; the signal of course had long been given, as when Rimbaud wrote *Je est un Autre* and when Laforgue echoed him with *Je m'ennui Natale.*

The stable ego of fiction had disintegrated—Lawrence says so in his letters; in every sector the basic propositions of theoretical physics had come under fire and some of these factors were of concern to poets—such as that one could not observe a field without disturbing it, so that all objective judgement was qualified. We had been taught to believe in the existence of absolute objective Truth—which would be revealed when analysis had gone far enough. But the new ideas made truth seem highly provisional and subject to scale and context. The Indians had always said that the notion of matter was an illusion, and *voilà* we had begun to find that this was becoming scientific fact. Not only physics—philosophy and psychology were also in an impasse, thanks to Freud. He had deciphered Hamlet at last, and we now knew his madness to be our own. Both the outside world and the inner one had been quite transformed by these ideas. Of course long ago the Indians had told us that the notion of the discrete and separate ego was also an illusion—perhaps a dangerous one. Under the probings of Freud and Co. it had all but disintegrated already! Here again the Asiatics seemed to be right. Hamlet's father's ghost had emerged once more upon the stage.

I am simplifying this matter now, and of course when I was twenty I had not fully grasped it in detail. Now I see that the fashionable critical notion of 'two cultures' is a misconceived one. All the great poets who took the European spirit as a responsibility were fully abreast of this crisis. Valery studied mathematics, Eliot was familiar with the precepts of Patanjali, Rilke and Yeats also; while in the greatest of them Fernando Pessoa, we find a lucid exposition of the crisis which led to so many hysterical symptoms like Dada and Surrealism, to mention only two.

This for me was a great problem as I felt that I needed some sort of classical frame upon which to expose the tapestry which I wanted to weave. I did not know whether I could use some of the by-products of this crisis and use them as if they were classical unities. The disintegration of the stable ego, the subject-object relationship, the poetic sickness of syntax which made modern poetry so like the effusions of talented schizophrenics. . . . Could I make myself a classical backcloth out of the by-products of relativity?

The worst was that there was nobody with whom I could discuss such matters; they did not interest people, and I knew no poets. Had I been less of a fool, had I passed my exams and gone to Oxford things would have been different. But I didn't. I was like a cat taken and left miles from home—I was really trying to find my way back to India. It was not clear of course, but now I see it was really that. It led me to become a European to begin with—at eighteen I was footloose in Europe. My father gave me some money to spend on books and travel. It was not much, I travelled like a poor student, with a rucksack. How marvellous it was! I discovered Greece at twenty-one.

In this country I discovered the Ancient Greek philosophers like Heraclitus and discovered their Indian parentage, for there was hardly one who had not studied his philosophy in India. I was half way home, and to celebrate this I wrote the *Black Book*. I was influenced by surrealism but not convinced theoretically. It did not really touch my deeper preoccupation with form, and the rupture of form by science. Forms in the novel since Proust had become circular, as if they were trying to darn the hole. Time or memory now extended into infinity. We had believed that the history of man began with Adam and Eve, but the new geology extended time immeasurably. We thought that the *Iliad* was a folklore poem; Schleimann uncovered the remains of Troy and proved it a reality. After Freud it was not possible again to write Hamlet. The universe had become a huge incomprehensible machine from which the only philosophy to be drawn was one of cosmic pointlessness.

And man? His coherence and self-possession had become dispersed and tarnished by doubts about his identity. Was he simply a succession of states, like an old movie? Once more one thought of the Indian notions about human identity . . .

It seemed to me that if I could somehow touch all this in a novel it would need stereoscopic vision and stereophonic sound, not to mention jump-cutting like a modern film. The matter would be the ordinary old-fashioned matter for novels, people and situations and quotidien problems—but all seen through this new angle of vision. I was much helped in these ideas by Wyndham Lewis's book *Time and Western Man*. He was the only English intellectual who was actively interested in these ideas which were fermenting in Europe at the time. It is very hard to interest the English writer in ideas.

I went to live in Greece, a very dangerous course for a young writer, as it cut me off from literary life in London altogether; I had met nobody, neither editors nor publishers nor other writers—which is the normal way to begin a career in letters. But I needed this country very badly in order to hatch the eggs I wanted to lay. In those days Greece was, from the European point of view, not only primitive and dangerous, but a long way away. So much so that when first my poems received any notice I was treated as an English 'Gaugin' in an article by Derek Stanford! Now everyone has visited this beautiful, modern, prosperous little country.

At first I was very much alone, but in a few years I acquired, by a series of pure flukes, a number of uncles or godfathers or whatever you may call them; benevolent spirits to guide my path, to judge my work. I was electrified when they told me that I had something more than juvenile promise. I am so vain that the more I am praised the better I work. These great men, some of whom were then unknown, gave me the necessary encouragement to persevere. What luck! I discovered that T. S. Eliot was my editor; among other uncles I had Henry Miller, George Seferis, George Katsimbalis the Colossus of Maroussi, and Theodore Stephanides the great savant, doctor, astronomer, biologist, cancerologist—everything! I could not have hoped for such a circle of acquaintance had I gone on living in suburban London. And at 22 years of age! I was not too stupid not to recognise the importance of these friendships. Among them was one aunt, the delectable Anaïs Nin. I shall never forget that when I arrived in Paris a couple then completely unknown came to the station to meet me and praise me for the

Black Book—Anaïs Nin and Henry Miller! They brought me as a gift, Otto Rank's *Art and Artist*, right there to the station. We went to the Café Dôme for a drink.

Paris as usual was humming with ideas, like a beehive, and here at last I found people with whom I could discuss these ideas—albeit in the shadow of the swastika, for the war had almost arrived. Yet the portrait I had sketched of our intellectual predicament proved to be accurate—both the outside world, the world of matter, and the inside world, the world of the self, had been completely transformed by advances in science. As for atomic physics the very language used today to try and describe the debris of the atom—for it has disintegrated into some two hundred sub-particles, is taken from Joyce and reminds one of Lewis Carrol. As the particles become increasingly diminutive in size and enigmatic in function a kind of literary hysteria set in; the smallest so far have been christened 'quarks' a word borrowed from Joyce. A quark has three forms, 'up' 'down' and 'strange'. This is not all. They have another quality which the same looking-glass minds have christened 'charm'. Finally, to complicate the picture further, they must be considered as either 'top' or 'bottom' and to have yet another quality called 'spin'. The first DADA manifesto is nothing to this extraordinary parade of scientific categories borrowed from literature! Poor Joyce! Even though his Finnegan, a real curiosity of literature, is really a potentially protracted pun! The important thing for me was the dissolution of the fiction of the stable discrete ego. Despite the apparent originality of Freud's discoveries the majority of his ideas had been anticipated years before by another Viennese doctor, whose work while popular, did not cause the same sort of revolution. His name was Von Feuchtersleben. We see I think from this that each great man is really a syndicate of several other great men. He matches and accords dissimilar views and finds a new synthesis from old ideas. He is a joiner and harmoniser more than an inventor. There is no need to go further with this sort of exposition; the question was this: could such material influence literary form, and provide a sort of frame? It was certainly more topical and more typically modern than so much which the modern novel was treating.

I began to dream of a sort of novel-as-apparatus (*un roman-appareil*) which one could use as a historic or poetic 'conscience', as portable as a pocket-compass! I did not wish (even had I ever had the talent) to build a word-cathedral like Joyce; you must be a dispossessed Catholic for that. I wanted to build something like a cave-cooperative with perhaps Dionysus as manager!

It was years before I dared to begin on such a book, and meanwhile I went into training for the big fight by learning how to write. I wrote in many different styles and on many topics. I felt that not only the world was coming to an end but also language—for the new visual age had begun to arrive. I felt that one day we should communicate in grunts like black jazzmen! I was too pessimistic I now see, but nevertheless the trend is still apparent. But side by side with this merely scientific interest I was also reading the Upanishads translated by Yeats, and discovering the Chinese philosophers who one day would teach me their magic, which is the art of manipulating the inevitable! What seemed evident to me was that all disciplines, all styles, were gradually moving closer to each other, whether East and West, or simply mysticism and logic. It has not gone as fast or as far as I expected but already in this contemporary world the trend has become a marked one.

I am not sure, but I think there is a faint hope of a great synthesis which will conjoin all fields of thought, however apparently dissimilar, to making them interpenetrate, interfertilise. This is the sense in which it is worth being a poet. We must learn from such doctor-mystics as Groddeck to treat the whole of reality as a symptom!

I went back to Greece to wait for the coming of the expected war. I took Miller with me for a holiday. In this Greek island one felt very strongly that ancient Greece had its roots in

Egypt, whence India. For my part I also had one foot in Vienna, so to speak, with Freud and Jung and Groddeck. I began to see what becoming a European meant!

While I was wondering about this, the Germans made a useful contribution to my thinking by chasing me all the way down Greece, into Crete, and thence into Egypt. I would have been too lazy to visit Alexandria myself—I was not interested in Egypt, I was happy in Greece. But in Alexandria I found myself at the cradle from which the whole of our civilisation had sprung. The roots of all our theologies as well as the roots of mathematics and physics had been hatched here. The first measurements of the earth—something as exciting as going to the moon—had been made here. Between Plotinus, Philo and Euclid all aspects of human thought had been enriched here. It was the ideal frame for a book which might try, in a modest way, to touch the contemporary reality. It was impertinent, I suppose, to invoke the Gods, like Einstein and Freud, but that was the way I saw things, and I was quite pleased when in the book I saw the stereo effects, and the slight bending of time and space—like Einsteinian space being curved!

The success was astonishing and very pleasing; I was amply rewarded for the thought and reflection which had gone into the book.

Nothing has changed today in the world picture, but what is apparent is that the two metaphysics, Eastern and Western, are moving steadily together and given time will meet in many essential fields. Numen and phenomenon were made to be complementaries and not opposites. It is so obvious that this is happening that I decided two years ago to celebrate this marriage, which I foresaw, by making a small group of novels, interlaced and interdependent based on the five-power system of the Buddhist psychology—the five aggregates, so to speak. A five-part book, independent but linked in a new way, a somewhat haphazard way, but occupied with much the same material as the last. One's experience of life is very limited. In this book I proposed to return to India—to move from the four dimensions to the five skandas. The old stable ego had already gone, reality has realised itself there, so to speak. In a sense all my new people are aspects of one great person, age, culture. I would like to make a metaphor for the human condition as we are living it now. I have dug sideways also to make a tunnel back into the Quartet, for part of the action of this new novel takes place in Egypt, and one meets characters and places from the old Quartet, but they are not named. But passionate fans —*les fervents*—will recognise them. I like to think that there is a family feeling about my books and here and there a character from an early book may stray into a later book without warning. I like this sort of continuity which hints at an inner progression from the *Black Book* onwards. I need two more years for the last three books. I am not of course sure that my idea will work, but if it does I will have two floating structures, poems of celebration drawn from the East and the West. Imagine two Calder-mobiles. After that I shall be happy to retire. I have a few things more to say about the destiny of woman, the fate of the world and the second law of thermodynamics—the law of divine entropy. I would like to say them as an Indian this time!

Time and causality have very much preoccupied our age, and science has so much overflowed into the field of artistic creation that it has provided new forms, new moulds for the fiery magma. Proust, Joyce were both time-intoxicated artists, soaked in history and the historic consciousness. They were hunting for the Nunc Stans, the permanent Now of the philosopher.

Often effects and causes seem not to be joined, not to depend on each other, when it is simply that the distance is too great to discern the connection. Yet they are.

Once upon a time Aristotle, who only pronounced upon nature when he was sure of the truth of his statements asserted *Natura non Facit Saltis*, thus upholding the unbroken chain of causality. '*Nature does not do Anything in Jumps*'. It moved in orderly process, link by link, respecting a perfect determinism—that is how he saw it. Then after two thousand years Darwin timidly, haltingly puts down in his private notebook a tentative repudiation of this flat assertion. He writes: 'One species does not *change* into another, it does so at one blow, *per saltum*'. The jump! It was a treacherous thought to harbour for it compromised the rigid determinism of the pure Aristotelian thought. Nature could jump, nature could if she wanted syncopate! Quanta!

I like to compare these two views of reality in symbolic terms by imagining the contrast between a European cathedral and an Asiatic pagoda; my own word-pagoda is to have five faces. But the cathedral is built like a boat or a bird; you have to enter it to reach its centre of gravity which is the altar which an Asiatic would see as a sort of telephone booth. By putting in the right coin (prayer) one could contact God, the presiding personage or principle, and bargain with him. The altar is the bar or the counter at which the transaction takes place, where your soul is tested for its qualities and defects. Heaven and hell are the two possibilities which are offered to it; bliss or eternal anguish. It is a very simple and brutal view of the human option; moreover among the extreme dangers or sins is human sexuality. Well, the cathedral seems to have had its day. Once they were prayer-factories generating good behaviour and a kindly disposition towards men; now they seem like out of work computers. The belief in Christian prayer has been very much eroded. It seems to have been replaced by a communal will to unhappiness which I think we can read into our architecture which breathes confinement, regimentation, heralds of insanity. If this goes on within a short time it will be hard to decide whether a building is a residence or a barrack or a factory or an insane asylum . . . They are getting to look so alike.

By contrast to this attitude, the five skanda pagoda mind, which has begun to enjoy a great vogue, is perhaps equally full of traps though for us it seems to represent a blissfully calm view of reality. This is because it seems to offer a relief from materialist thought. The non-ego attitude is its ideal, and its science emphasises the insubstantiality of matter, and posits a kind of energy over mass state of mind which perhaps is what Einstein really meant, for he was as deeply religious in a pantheistic way as Newton!

I am trying to move in my selfish and hesitating way from the fourth dimension to the five skanda view, using the same old equipment of the domestic novel, as a kaleidoscope uses the same bits of glass for different patterns. I would like to try and use the by-products of Asiatic philosophy as I tried in the Quartet to use the by-products of relativity philosophy. I think the new form I am chasing will be less schematic and more floating, to fit the oriental notion of reality; slowly already some of the characters who only exist in the imagination of the others, are coming on to the stage to compromise the orthodox ideas of 'reality'. I wonder if it will work satisfactorily, and produce a group of books which satisfy as an organic whole? In this new Asiatic domain the passport is the 'mandala' (which Jung kept finding in the unconscious of his patients!). It's a sort of cardiagram of the human being's destiny. My cast is more or less the same—the two women blonde and dark, two clowns, lovers, poets, warriors, monks, villains and seers. The old stuff of fiction and Christmas pantomime, under different names. Looked at in this way one should ask oneself not if they are 'real' but if they are 'true'; that is to say true to this prismatic poetic reality. A single individual's experience of people and places is extraordinarily limited, and if he is an artist he feels forced to accept these limitations and do his best within them. But certain sharp contrasts of a formal kind will impose themselves; the moving staircase of the 'linear' progression will be replaced by something closer to the 'flying carpet' of the fairy tales. And people? They will be spare parts of one another from the cosmic point of view, though quite real and discrete from a worldly, novelistic point of view. Underneath the action will I hope be the Asiatic notion of a world renewed afresh with each thought; therefore man as a Total Newcomer to each moment of time. It will need readers indulgent to this rather sphinx-like way of thinking; but then the 'real' reader has always known that he or she must read between the lines. That is where the truth hides itself. Process in scientific terms is irreversible, though not in Asiatic, while truth as such is ambivalent. The sages appear to have co-opted it successfully for use as a pivot, so that it gives cosmic balance to the human animal. It would be a wonderful thing to feel that, having paid my respects to Europe and its relativity principle in the Quartet, I could now, as my star is sinking, touch my forelock to the Indian view of life. I would like to plant this Quintet at the point of tangence between these two cultural principles, so that it could be fruitful as well as entertaining.

In conclusion it is worth stressing that all the abstract symbols one uses in a disquisition of this kind—words like 'relativity' or 'Tao' or 'matter' or 'Maya' are to be regarded as road-signs which indicate the density and direction of the intellectual traffic. They are not absolutes. I imagine that the sage considers them to be simply the paint rags upon which the artist wipes his brushes once the painting is complete. We must not let philosophy become a self-caressing machine.

George Barker

FOR GASCOYNE'S 65TH BIRTHDAY

Drawing by George Barker

By what I am moved to give this word to you
David both of us know, but it is not simply to send you
a card with a nosegay for your sixty-fifth birthday
although I would offer you every lucky memento:
no, it is the sense that what I offer comprises
an invasion of your spiritual isolation,
that isolation, David, so like an Isola Bella
or that garden where the sleeping imagination
serenely dreams that it need never waken.
What I seek to learn from you I know to be not
that answer to a question but, above all else, the
affirmation within your always lucid silences
like the silence of Donatello. Only those statues know
how to affirm elucidations that speech
would somehow degrade into obscure or strident
approximations or guesses. These we can leave
to the fashionable riff raff and rhetoricians.
What I am moved to put to you here and now
as we both walk towards the blackwater river
is the proposition that even Augustine can seem
sometimes to be the two-handed instrument
of what we have no better word for than evil.
'All Nature, inasmuch as it is nature,
is good.' What, then, David, is the origin of this evil
if not an impulse of the natural man?
Or is this natural man exempt from evil
like earthquakes, India, or the divine intention?
You have spent long nights in the cave of origins
where thoughts hang like the dismembered limbs of heroes
and now, I think, you know that all thought is illusion.
The natural man David dances before the sacred
altar and hearth within the original cave.

Erwin Castillo

(Would the author kindly send us his address?)

TIRADORES DE MUERTE

I

Good-bye forever, as though finality, all magnificence
And bronze, existed in the piteous wood of possibilities.
True. Summer is a barbarous event: widowed gumamelas groan

And wave their bony arms; they've stumps where hearts should be.
The once-wicked cock of the mountain yields to the harquebuss
Crowing (acting an irony): 'Easy it came and now easy it goes!'

2

All the Armies of Spain march on our mountain!
We, Tiradores de Muerte, are mustered like flies
Upon the entrails of the murdered hawk of Cavite.
The Spanish chew iron and spit cannonballs at us.
They fire muskets at the dome of our tribal tree.
Their guidons are erect, poised to rape the skies
And Death is a telegraph wire beribboned with moss.

3

Mountain! I love her!

Her eyes are deep
onyx lakes in the midnight
where jamines and the Three Marys
swoon away to swim.
Wild winds
delirious with flowers
make caravels of her blown hair.
For her elf-ear
they sing and the fine down
stirs between her breasts.
Her face is pale as a pearl from the South.
Her tongue, snake-quick, lights in my mouth.
She then says Good-bye forever.

Mountain: I love her and I am afraid!

4

Young children, look, for there are lessons in the legend.
Death, but love also, lurk in the ardent wood of possibilities
And metal nightmares bear the Tiradores off to meet them
Whom we will greet with anthems and with torches.

A LANDSCAPE FOR THE BRIDE

This is our three-spoked cross.
That round of lake is its deep head.
By the roadside, my aunts sprout like mushrooms;
They have palm-wine, fruits of globed sunshine in their baskets.

The wind rasps like a guitar that had wept all night.
It sang the vanished horsemen on their way: the coughing heroes
With long swords, off to join Rosal, or another furious chief
Whose hunting horn had roused them from death's sleep.

Cholera and earthquake will come again to our high hills,
And from some huts take four or five as roughage for the earth:
In the town of the Alapaap, few are the homes that will be spared.

KUNG 'DI MAN

Flee away now: I shroud my eyes to your departure:
The harvest browns upon the plain and strong lads
Hoist a Maytime chant you cannot long endure.

And so it ends: it will not keep till the moon wanes:
Frail and precious, no amulet could have borne it safe
Through this lucid place more treacherous than cannons.

No, do not sear the wound with words to raise a decorative scar.
Frail and precious, it shapes after its image gentle memorials,
And bells in the evening comment on the sadness of the weather.

And what it was we shared, I can scarce recall: we journeyed
Down a highway without towns or landmarks, and briefly once
Suffered my mouth to touch a pain that coiled there unannounced.

Benoy Chakraborty

(Chakraborty is a young Indian poet who lives in Beauregard, France, with his two daughters. *Watermarks*, a collection of his poetic prose illustrated with delicate engravings by Frank Connelly was published by The Lyrebird Press in 1973.)

BEAUREGARD

The trees in the courtyard are old;
Stendthal probably sat under these chestnuts
On his way to the town or napped as I do
Under this centurion Linden in the warm afternoon
Sneezing with a pinch of the voluptuous snuff.
Fresh lichen of the spring is silken over the cistern
Moist like the labia of desire and to darkness returned.
And the holly oak on whose magistral timber
Someone slashed an arrow in a heart
Cogitates since the time of Descartes.
Only the leaves are new against the blue of the sky
Fresh like Persian miniatures.

If you sit too long you dissolve
Wash upon wash in warm lava of colours.
There is no measure of time here
Not in days or years
Or in all those constructs funded through hope or fear
Of self-fulfilling prophecies.
Only now dimly do I perceive the Newtonian wheel
Of action and reaction of unspent momentum of the will.
Karmā has its own inertia its own logic of sorrow.
Reversing the sign of the arrow will alter nothing.
What has happened will happen again.
What will happen had already happened.
Between past and future there is a symmetry
Almost identical as the two sides of the tapestry.

Sitting under this shade-bearing tree
You learn to live in that timeless moment
Of ripening of detachment from the branch
Oblivious of the fall. To be absorbed
Into this moment here and now
Is all. Like the arrow finally released from the bow
From the tension of the spring.
Clockwork of the will is finally dismantled
With its hysteria of desire pulling the puppet-string
To viennese waltz. No more urge
For analytic prescriptions in the anatomy
Of dreams disfigured through scrutiny.

As if flesh can be scoured or innocence purged.
I see desire flashing by below and beyond
The wile of the angling mind over the pond,
Slipping easily past the net of intentions.
Manic mind in division must heal
Through joining like palms in prayer or by fusion
Unto bodies warm like loaves or wanton
In surfeit of tenderness.

Flesh is both thorn and flowering.
Love in the prescience of pain. But mostly love
Even at the moment of the darkening sphere.
I do not know for sure. But so did I hear her whisper
When the body had become slight and tormented
Like a shuttle in the wind and her voice
Soft notes of the angelus ebbing near and far
That 'Love is a moving moving train and
Lovers must not linger in the corridor of pain
And I can hardly wait to become leaves and rain.'

Time is the sound from the Bell-fry
Down in the village. Or in the plumage of the jet
Or of the motionless falcon in the sky.
In its eyes of polished stone
I too am reflected as he in mine
Till in the twin reflection through the lens of space and time
You do not know if the two of us the double
Are not a flaw of vision, in the gem;
That the dreamer and the dream like the seer and the seen
Is not the same as the predator with the prey
In the moment of undivided attention.

Expanding rings of time as the space confines
Like lips around kisses unrendered. Delivered
To here and now like this seigneurial seat
By miracle. Pray for those who missed
The present by a hair's breath. Living is being
From instant to instant of recognition.
Being is burning in every moment like these hot lilacs
Over the escarpments of flint.
And in the shifting cat's eye of the instinct
The dark meniscus of the unerring self.
And year after year
As these old chestnuts and the ancient lime
Turn into leaves and snow and feather
Searching and shedding the lineaments of time
The soliloquy of the heart-broken lover,
Returns to this point of the first coincidence

Where love could almost have been.
  And to the sightless spirit of the place
The returning nightingale plays
Once more the timeless melody of silence.

Dick Davis

READING

The last page read you pat
With thoughtful tenderness
  Your novel's spine—
How much I'm moved by that
Improbable caress
  Which I thought mine.

I copied it from you?
You picked it up from me?
  Who knows which way
The gentle gesture flew . . .
It marks that privacy
  We both obey.

Richard Eberhart

GRANDSON

And while I was waiting
For my grandchild to exclaim again,
I thought of my age,
And of his young sophistication.

Born into a world of professors
As the century waned,
What direction would society
Take in his time?

Such high intelligence!
Such delight of life!
But what will it come to,
Death is the knife

Will part him from his predecessors
And who can say what adventure
Will open to him
The twenty-first century?

Dear three-year-old, dear man,
What can I say to you
But love and affirmation,
And my elan

In face of obstacles,
In face of death's derision,
That I was like you
Daft with vision?

THE HOP-TOAD

The hop-toad jumped away, missing the blade,
When Betty was mowing the garden.
She instinctively said, I beg your pardon.

G. S. Fraser

(These are possibly the last poems by G.S.F. which will appear in PL. He died in January 1980 and we are grateful to his wife, Paddy, for them.)

LOVE POEM

In a reposing hand
White like the perfect snows
My hand now lies, and one
Resourceful as the rose,

Unmitigated grace
On which to concentrate
My hunted, haunted gaze:
Still trapped by Time too late,

Since careless Beauty that
I saw and did not see
Winds up my loose-skeined days
Round neat Eternity:

Lost, unlost, light retold,
Unfold, refold surprise.
Snow, snow. Snow rose.
Of smoky campfire eyes.

Long is your path and mine
Twines off and gently fades,
But unafraid. Dark wine
Shall warm me in the Shades.

ADAM AND EVE

That lovely animal was rational
Though all the dumb appealing of her eyes
Spoke of confusion more than of the Fall.
He could have torn the fig leaf from her thighs.
Lust which had cast out fear, had brought in shame.
There was that Flaming Sword between them still.
Though they forgot the Angel and his name

He stood heraldic on that bald, low hill.
Of eating Knowledge ignorant ecstasy
Had come: the strong pulse promising an end.
Still on his tedious tapestry stood He,
Posing. They waited for him to descend,
And waiting grasped what the manoeuvre meant:
The Choice in waiting was the Punishment.

A LOVER'S QUARREL

Now I have smashed it finally, I think.
And such sad harshness in her stare.
Eyes seemed wet stone. And yet I drink
Life from her love as from the air.
Caught as half-throttled at the very brink
Of no more breathing, of the air withdrawn,
No use, it seemed, to cry or rant or fawn,
All gesture frozen into falsity
Of, in that gaze, the knowledge of false me,
Seen as not here, that never had been there.
Then her hand touches mine, and I exist.
It was hurt, healing love and not despair.
Salt was the reconciling taste we kissed.
And my tears salt on hyacinthine hair.

Rivka Fried

(The first three poems describe the spiritual struggle of the poet who was born in Israel and educated in Tel Aviv and New York. She lives in London today and is a free-lance journalist and writer. T.)

ISRAEL: A BETRAYAL

I was born here, unknowing:
these eternal, metallic skies
and harsh sunlight on palm trees were a kind
of legacy. I drifted through forests
on the way to school with the others,
Tel Aviv was a rambling orchard then
and the righteousness they taught
tasted like dreams.

We were a realisation of history, they said,
like pegs on some nationalist wheel come
full circle, a sort of technology.
Reality was precise, defined by soldiers
and barriers. The night screams of coyotes
swallowed by planes and sirens.

The other, indigenous creatures were speechless
then, their own dreams still grasped
  in the black-crusted earth
  that once was Palestine.
I remember their watermelon shacks in summer:
the red fruit inside, easy brown faces,
wanting to touch the strangeness
on the periphery of a delineated life.
The women rustling like a conspiracy
in the dust of olive groves.

Ten years later the streets are rancid
with insurrection. The Jew turns oppressor:
another history lesson learnt.
And the earth unleashes its dark promise,
sprouting green-tufted guns and explosives
in the groves and terraced fields.

1978

NEW JERUSALEM

It's a sign, a symbol of resurrection
following the wind-swept desolation.
A myth spawned in the vicissitudes
  of consciousness:
at the unguarded hour multitudes
are leaving for Jerusalem:

the exodus in the roads of my dreams.
And five years later, I repeat the question:
these faces are known, there must be a lesson.
But why Jerusalem (that hardened city
  bruised with trampled stone)
Can one choose the rabbis, or pray alone

is method born of disintegration.
Those that make it back never reply.
I dream of a returning lover matted
with beard: an over-due prophet.
His new growth pronounces the only
testimony of a silent journey.

Also women, familiar and painful
  are departing
slowly as in dreams with sparse belongings.
With night the scenes flicker, like road
signals to a single destination.
Jerusalem is a sign, we're told

a symbol of resurrection.
Perhaps the lesson is in discerning:
the passage and the discarding.

1981

ROOTS
(Mediterranean Revisited)

From the air just soft spring
night and city lights;
unprompted tears ripping
through aircraft anonymity.
Crossing the border an old
presence engulfs me painlessly
like eternal skin.
These roots know no agony.
The landscape all dust and silver.

And alive; the nodding rocks
almost green with wild flowers.
Drops of anemones rushing
like something primeval, maybe blood;
walking down mountain roads
sparks of myself flaring
from cypress groves and ridges of stone.
The same reflections in the water.
Some life was submerged in

the detachment of Europe.
Now the olive blossoms and sun
scorch me bone-clean as the cliff face.
The mind's foot prints are indelible
like unobtrusive plants with
roots deeply grounded. There is
continuity. In the dead pain
of northern winter I lived on
in these groves and silver silence.

IN MEMORY OF THE OLD MAN
(Gordon Fraser)

For many, you somehow marked the seasons;
a name conjuring feast-days and time passing.
Those who came closer recall the preserved
humane face of material success;
an old man whose sweeping enthusiasms

sputtered with adjectives like 'fabulous'.
For myself, it was simplistic grandeur
reposing among fig trees and white light
on your provencal verandah last Easter.
You sat, a solitary yet full figure

wild crutches in the air gesticulating
the force of your exuberant convictions.
Towards your death I recall a lonely face
at a lamp-lit dinner table waiting.
You weren't the sort to go gently

that good night over-powered suddenly:
a morning on the English motorway.
Old man, my poetry never captured
you in your lifetime: those formless stanzas
thin as ashes circling over Provence.

Angie Gilligan

RETURNING FROM WAR

Returning from war, Boris was strange.
He sat flat-eyed watching the roses
and would not come out of his room.

'The killing' sighed his mother
'The cruelty' wept his downy wife

and they whispered their feet through the house.

'Not cruelty' said Boris,
'Those who killed best
were the meek and the mild mannered
who were quiet and polite to their neighbour
who respected the doctor
and the bank manager
who had great respect for the judge
who sat, small-eyed, in the clerk's seat of peace.

When they were told—
"Today and today and today you shall kill"
they bent their hands to guns and bombs
and made everything heavy with dying.

It was the curiousness of death
how casually it came
and the space between life and skin
not a crash but a murmur
for the red to seep
and the heart jolt still.

Knowing this—nowhere is safe,
everywhere is smooth and perilous.
Knowing this—is like always walking naked
into snow'.

Pull-out opposite: Poem *Hands* by Bryan Guinness illustrated by John Piper.

BATHSHEBA

Bathsheba in mourning
for her love her dear one
places the sugar in the teapot
and sprinkles her cereal
with salt.

Oh he has become dark and unyielding
as a tomb of twenty horses.

At work she neglects
to stamp the post
and cannot invent replies
when questioned.

Night he stumbles in
late and drunk.
He would be where he is not
and so makes gruff remarks
about the mounting dust
and who has fed the cat.

In bed he makes fierce nothing
to her.
Vigorous and brief.

Quietly in the dark
she lets loose tears
the size of pennies
and morning wears her tee shirt
inside out.

John Heath-Stubbs

POEM

Polyphemus weeps
Into the Straits of Messina—
The monster, who does not know
Why he is so unloved
Except by his woolly sheep;
Why brisk Galatea flouts him, or why
Ruthless No-one has burned away
His solitary eye.

His father a Mediterranean storm,
His mother an anonymous nymph—
An unpromising background; he haunts
Pine-shaggy uplands, or where
The pumice fragments are strewn
In the burnt-out crater of Aetna.

Polyphemus died, of cramps and cold.
Nobody knows where his bones were laid.
But when bones were dug up
In fourteenth century Sicily
Boccaccio opined:
'The bones of Polyphemus!'
But the learned world has settled
For paleontology, an elephant.

Mike Jenkins

NIGHT SWIMS SLOWLY

White blossoms curtain the slopes
keeping night in the wings.
The vines on their terraces
are bare wires awaiting the sun's connection.

There are no seagulls in the air's net.
But this promenade, with its hotels
bright as light-ships, has wave
after wave of revellers, arms linked.

As we sit, buoyed with conversation
swilled wine rocking the valley,
their blurted and jarring songs
are like orders anchoring the evening.

Across the river, lights of a village
bead the neck of a slope.
Night swims slowly into the valley
and the moon is afloat.

As party-goers stumble, our smiles
tip the river seaward to where breakers
grate their teeth, and the wind
would twist hair into rope.

Elizabeth Jennings

NEUTRAL

It had been simple in the past but now
You seemed to unlearn one another and
Like strangers stare, like enemies, too, stand,
But, worse than this, is that you can't think how

It felt to be each other's energy,
Each other's wish, no self-demanding but
An opening of every door once shut
In mind, in senses. What huge enemy

Hinted at war? But beyond battles is
Being and feeling neutral. Would you have
Infidelity and true distress
To make you touch again the quick of love?

Peter Johnson

GEORGE STUBBS

Who would guess this passionate man
Strung horse carcases up, stinking
His studio with their flesh.
Like a watchful surgeon
Sat patiently devouring
Each line of the dead beast
For our favoured mansions.

And dragging the bones and flesh
On to the exquisite canvas
With ferocious honesty,
He plants these great animals,
Fiery eyed Gods, among
Their puny owners, wives,
And elegant quiet fields
In the evening light;
Before putting them out to grass,
His loving anatomy done.

FOR AN OLD MAN DYING IN HOSPITAL

This mad old wanton heart
Palsied with trying,
Lecherous, too clapt out for love,
Brought near to death, heart failing, crying,
With the morticians waiting
For his exsanguinate corpse.
On the slab, post-mortem,
'Aortic valve deformed
The pox has got him'.

Who will reprove these bent bones
Whose only fault was living
Blind to his zodiac and his seasons.
Once lusty boy with eyes for loving
Frosted apple or gold breasted
Girl whom Renoir would have fancied.

Now in a last fierce breath,
Lonely and quinsied,

Ardently calls upon his Gods,
Forgotten now the ancient faith
Without a blush from the old bones.
And from his mask, toothless and queer
In its recent beauty
Forces a pagan prayer.

So, shall we teach him his beads
In this seven starred fever?
Or let him die sinful and sweet
In his black bed forever.

Keith Jones

THE SEER

But you man you what do you own?
Body? O no. We've picked that bone clean.
O yes. I mean it's so umbilically funny.
You   dear miss grasping little orifice
My patient pecked at pecking hen
Eggs hatchway to another egg   you
Are an absolute structure
A hairy soft machine without a ghost

But mind man mind? O no. That's blown.
We are possessed by memory and not
Our own. It is not the thing we name
The flower that twinges you   the
                    woman's spore
But histories of it that resume in us
The fuss along the corridors   excitement
                    in the cells
And here's the word working at the mouth
And here is someone else's language
                    speaking us

FORCE

She is Omen's daughter drenched
In white saying to herself where
The black water ends
Endings are white. They bleed you.
Those white muffled blows

In this cold cauldron
This drag and carry or water water
That wind raising a weal of rain
On the horizon tousling the palms
Slapping rings in the water
These are my familiars
I do not understand the rocks
They are not my kind of survival
I only know I mean to be me
But that it hurts to only be
Moving only to be moved
To fall in on myself until the mind
Explodes like white grenades

The lion roars and eats my hands
Inside him now I am safe

Grevel Lindop

RAIN ON RYDAL WATER

Like the human face
rain on water has its three perspectives,
each as relative
as profile, full-face, three-
quarter view, an arbitrary
breaking to aspects
by the angle of sight:

away in front of you
a flickering net, milk-white
shaking on metalbright water;
near at hand circles
intersecting circles intersecting
circles; and to your right a dazzle of
sparks, needlepoint
glints splintering the surface,

rushing in to attack
the monumental, bracken-red
image of a mountain
that muses in weightless silence
under the surface-trouble
of each drop coming home for the billionth time

to annihilation, adding its tiny quantum
to the depth of that spacious mirror.

Christopher Logue

THE AARDVARK

Into the moonlit midnight,
out of his stateless hole,
set for an insect intake,
a common Aardvark stole.

Depict a common Aardvark:
globe eyes of fiery rose;
long of ear, of tongue, of tail;
yet longer still of nose.

He sniffs the ermine moonshine.
He hears the vermin snore.
Brisk as a whip the Aardvark's tongue
streaks from the Aardvark's maw . . .

GIGANTIC LICK SNUFFS GLOW-WORM!
MIDGE-CLOUD ENGULFED MID-AIR!
followed by half-a-thousand ants,
(an Aardvark's normal fare),

a myriad of rotifers
cruising a humid nit,
another half-a-thousand ants,
(to keep him fat but fit),

an ounce of infant locusts,
a cashe of millipedes,
another half-a-thousand ants,
and then?—ah, then he needs

rest on the trek through hunger
to woo his mortal soul.
Meekly the common Aardvark
goes back into his hole.

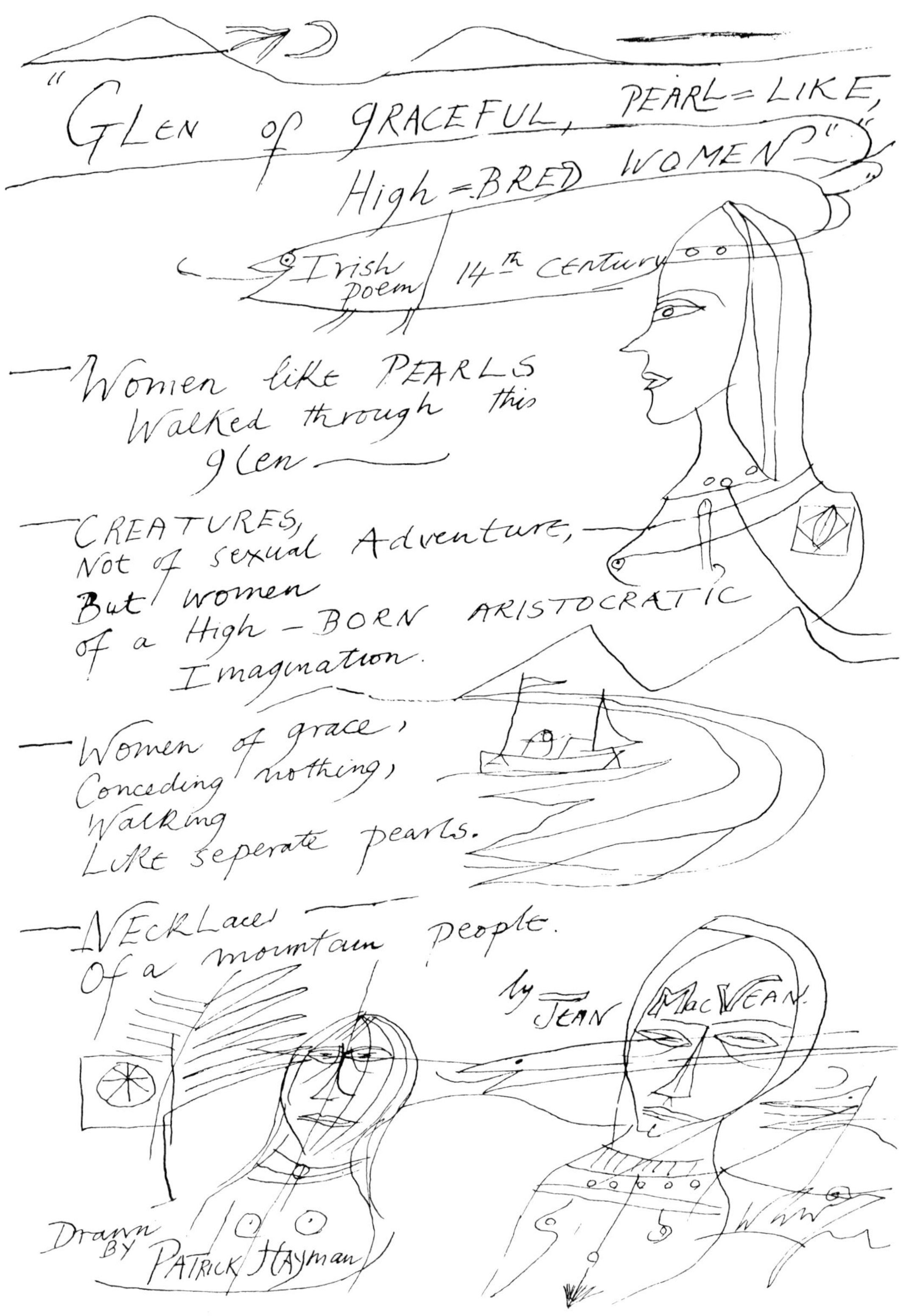
"GLEN of GRACEFUL, PEARL-LIKE,
High-BRED WOMEN"
Irish poem / 14th century
—Women like PEARLS
Walked through this
glen—
—CREATURES,
Not of sexual Adventure,—
But women
of a High-BORN ARISTOCRATIC
Imagination.
—Women of grace,
Conceding nothing,
Walking
Like seperate pearls.
—NECKLaces
Of a mountain people.
by JEAN MacVEAN
Drawn BY PATRICK HAYMAN

Nicholas Moore

NODDING ON THE STROOMBIOUS

Strings in the earth and air,
  Wings in the sky and sea,
Stringy wings everywhere,
  Flying my mind from me
    —*Antiflatter of Flydom* (The Peek Anthology)

The nightingflails in silkworm wood
Are merrily on the make,
And may this gown that I'm wrapped in,
Mither, require no second-take.

Daughter, daughter, you didn't oughter
Declaim so disrespectful.
They only wants to see your eyes;
Of the rest they'll be neglectful.

Mither, mither, me milk-white chests
Are full of the gold of glory;
Why don't the roil photographers
Come and do something for me.

Me beamish lugs have much appal
And every bub is ghostly
As nowadizz the fashions izz,
And me mine is open mostly

O dochter, dochter, shot ye gab,
Your snail-sharp teetth are showing,
Your bleeding mind hangs out like a tongue
And your nothinggies are flowing.

Mithery, mithery, minus mo,
I thocht you'd go wherever I go;
All my in-sense I got from you;
All that I know I know you know . . .

And pootiful you be my love,
And beautiful, me darlin' darter,
Slim as the blokes in the old ash-grove
And the modernest self-starter.

Mum, ee, mum, ee, alas for me,
Me ingine's rinnin' doon,
And oo the ell can start me oop,
Woonce all the tits have floon

Ma sweet, ma sweet, ah'll fill thee bed
With sweets and candyfloss,
And when ye come for to be dead,
There'll be nae loss, there'll be nae loss.

There'll be nae loss abboot the hoose
In which nae sense li'd in;
There was no thong upon me mine
But to gae in and win.

But what I winnit wasnae nice;
It was in fact a burden,
So cheap, so tawdry, and precise
Beside the braes o'Auden.

O cratur, cratur, haud ye wist,
I wist ye are nae ma daughter.
So lay ye doon, cauld and unkissed
As all small craturs oughter.

Mither, O mither, mak ma bed soon
For ma grave is cold and creepy
And I only wished to show my mind
Before I grew too sleepy.

THE PASSIONATE YEARS
(or Just a Lack of Empson)

Sir William Empson

Laying claim to Auden, boys,
  What a lovely game,
Used to be the fashion, boys;
Now it's not the same.

Politics have faded and
  The eagle on the scarp
Feels a little jaded and
Has other things to hawk.

In the stooks the field-mice
  Cower amid detergent,
And the urge to yield nice
  Verse is not so urgent.

Empson's taut astringencies
  Are ladled out in prose.
No whiskers left to singe, as he's
  Master at least of those.

Young chaps have come along—cads
  Who know just what their game is.
We know where we went wrong, lads,
  Through never taking Amis.

And, when our guns we shot off
  Or tickled streams for pike,
We never got a lot of
  The properties we'd like.

O for the days of Auden
  And cleaner words, like 'snow',
Green fingers for the warden,
  And classics that we know;

When beards of Joyce and Ezra
  Gave pounds of kindly light,
And every *sich* was *besserer*,
  And day was Weill as night.

Laying claim to Auden, boys,
  Was such a lovely game.
But now there's not the passion, boys,
  And nothing's quite the same.

For these days are harum scarum
  And the passion's all for sects,
Mushrooms, space and Procol Harum
  And the gear that youth selects.

And the happy hunting fathers
  Or the victim on the ned
Aren't what really haunts and bothers
  Every shaggy little head.

GRAHAM SUTHERLAND

Graham Sutherland,
When he got to that other land,
Said:—'Thank God—but tell him I'm not
Accepting any more commissions of that kind because
of . . . well, you know what.'

PHILIP LARKIN

Philip Larkin
Said 'It'sh helluva dark in
Thish library tonight. And I'm afride
I can't even shee one little shimpering whitshun bride.'

Iris Murdoch

AGAMEMNON CLASS 1939

In Memoriam
Frank Thompson
1920–1944

Do you remember Professor
Eduard Fraenkel's endless
Class on the *Agamemnon*?
Between line eighty-three and line a thousand
It seemed to us our innocence
Was lost, our youth laid waste,
In that pellucid unforgiving air,
The aftermath experienced before,
Focused by dread into a lurid flicker,
A most uncanny composite of sun and rain.
Did we expect the war? What did we fear?
First love's incinerating crippling flame,
Or that it would appear
In public that we could not name
The aorist of some familiar verb.
The spirit's failure we knew nothing of,
Nothing really of sin or of pain,
The work of the knife and the axe,
How absolute death is,
Betrayal of lover and friend,
Of egotism the veiled crux,
Mistaking still for guilt
The anxiety of a child.
With exquisite dressage
We ruled a chaste soul.
They had not yet made an end
Of the returning hero.
The demons that travelled with us
Were still smiling in their sleep.

Heralded by the cries of hitherto silent Cassandra
The undulating siren creates in the entrails
And in the heart new structures
Of sensation, the abrupt start
Of war, its smell and sound.
The hours distend with bombs,
The big guns vibrate in the ground.
Frightened men kill by remote control
Or face to face appalled see their enemy fall.
Houses and public buildings with a kind of surprise
Bend their knees and turn into tombs.
Ever so many gentle worlds quietly end.
People sleep in catacombs.
White paths of doomed men
Daily criss-cross in the skies.
The sanctuary is bombed and lies
Open and unmysterious,
A garden of wild flowers.
Something crawls wounded on,
But the Holy One
Having suffered too long
Eventually dies.

Delphi medises and Apollo's face grows dim.
Was there a god there? We never saw him.
A priest was making a political sound.
Fey Helen lost her beauty and her shame,
Went home quite pertly in the end they say,
Piously helped the poor, became
A legend haunting a fought-over ground.
What was it for? Guides tell a garbled tale.
The hero's tomb is a disputed mound.
What really happened on the windy plain?
The young are bored by stories of the war.
And you the other young who stayed there
In the land of the past are courteous and pale,

Aloof, holding your fates.
We have to tell you it was not in vain.
Even grief dates, and even Niobe
At last was fed, and you
Are all pain and yet without pain
As is the way of the dead.
No one can rebuild that town
And the soldier who came home
Has entered the machine of a continued doom.
Only the sky and the sea
Are unpolluted and old

And godless with innocence.
And twilight comes to the chasm
And to the sea's expanse
And the terrible bright Greek air fades away.

JOHN SEES A STORK AT ZAMORRA

Walking among quiet people out from mass
He saw a sudden stork
Fly, from its nest upon a house.
So blue the sky, the bird so white,
For all these people an accustomed sight.

He took his hat off in sheer surprise
And stood and threw his arms out wide
Letting the people pass
Him by on either side
Aware of nothing but the stork-arise.

On a black tapestry now
This gesture of joy
So absolutely you.

Barbara Norman

GORILLA

(We are glad to print this poem by the late Barbara Norman, from her husband, Peter Ellson, along with the splendid portrait of her by Maeve Gilmore.)

The Hour has come
and there remains
one Eye alone—

Shall I clothe that Eye
with eyelash or with tear,
with love or lust?

Shall I set that jewel
in fair-faced flesh
for the curved bone
and the loved caress;
or shall I choose
this blackest hairiness,
making of love denial
that is bitterest?

Shall I draw near to stare
between those bars
that bind him from the stars,
and find behind the thrust
of anger, not coined hatred
minted from mistrust,
but the aching outrage
of a soul encaged.

Portrait by Maeve Gilmore

It would be less pain to take that black embrace,
than ever again to stare into eyes,
and find there the fair-faced lies of men.

Brian Patten

IN THE BED'S SHAPE HER SHAPE IS FORGOTTEN

——whose body has opened
Night after night
Harbouring loneliness,

Eating the emptiness
Of which I am made,
Night after night
Taste me upon you.

Night and then again night,
And in your movements
The bed's shape is forgotten.
Sinking through it I follow
Adrift on the taste of you.

I cannot speak clearly about you.
Night and then again night,
And after a night beside you
Night without you is barren.

I have never discovered
What alchemy makes
Your flesh different to the rest,
Nor why all that's commonplace
Comes to seem unique,

And though down my spine one answer leaks,
It has no way to explain itself.

THE MULE'S FAVOURITE DREAM

When the mule sings the birds will keep silent.
From among them they will choose a messenger,
He will fly to the court of the Emperor
And bowing with much decorum
Will complain bitterly.

And the Emperor, who until that moment
Had taken all songs for granted,
Will throw open the window and listening
Will detect in the mule's song
Some flaw of which he is particularly fond.

And he will say to the bird, 'O stupid thing!
Let the mule sing,
For there has come about a need of change,
There has come about
A need of magic things.'

This is the mule's favourite dream.
It is his own invention.
Deep in his brain's warren it blossoms.

ON TIME FOR ONCE

I was sitting thinking of our future
   and of how friendship had overcome
so many nights bloated with pain;

   I was sitting in a room that looked on to a garden
and a stillness filled me,
   bitterness drifted from me like frost, like dust.

I was as near paradise as I am likely to get again.

   I was sitting thinking of the chaos
We had caused in one another
   and was amazed we had survived it.

I was thinking of our future
   and what we would do together
and where we would go and how

   when night came
burying me bit by bit,
   and you entered the room,

trembling and solemn faced,
   on time for once.

Peter Porter

LITTLE HARMONIC LABYRINTH

Come stars and beg of the one star
a progress through the laughing fields
beyond our pink-walled town.
The little monkey on its cushion
brings the priceless gift
of sexual desire. Without this rubbing
luxury there'd be no chasseresse
of envy, nothing but our getting staler
on the avenues of evening.
How dare they share this gift,
these best of lucky solipsists—
'On this soft anvil all mankind was made.'
And the tyrant will,
unrepentent of its mediocrity,
is governor of created things.
The flight from meaning is our magic:
overhead a perfect line of birds
pegged out to dry—the picture shows
where dreams have passed,
trooping to a reborn god.
O captains of your consciences,
the world's a middle sea
washing tearful stories to the shore—
Tell of blushing psyches
in little breasts and sneakers
bringing serfdom to tomorrow,
reflate the fluffy trees, the cobalt sky
in allegories of sin,
with all our ages snickering in bushes.
Even the guaranteed untalented
have style of their own, our God
has given us immunity
from everything except ourselves.
No wonder I have dreamed
the living and the dead are one,
that out of their congestion
a planet rises which has sounds for air,
whose syntax can be synthesised.
O eyes I cannot meet,
yours, preppy teenage gods,
show me something serious
beyond imagination. When sex dries
all that's left is abstract.

completed outlines without presences.
     Find me a star
to shine through the whiteness of the mind.

PREPAREDNESS IS ALL

Fearing casualties, not in hundreds
but thousands or even millions,
the government ordered cardboard coffins
which could be folded quickly into shape
and stacked them ready
in every A.R.P. headquarters.

That was before we knew
'the fury of aerial bombardment'
goes differently. That was when death
was still individual,
no less foul and purposeless,
but waiting on a London Summer's day
coming out of doors to easy brightness.

There are places now where fire has passed,
worse than apprenticeships at Hiroshima.
There are lesions in imagination
which do not heal—and yet, some say,
show me a thing so terrible
it does not have a classic shrine
or moss-belaboured bower.

Genocide becomes a picture,
'Alexander at the Battle of Issus';
shock is when Miss Plath cuts her finger
and words like Red Brigades
ambush a reader's mind.

I will not let them flap through me.
Nothing is so quickly improvised
as history, an easy-to-assemble coffin.

Each head lies down in a burning bed.
We have been, we think, ourselves,
getting ready, getting ready . . .

'OLD AND ILL AND TERRIFIED AND TIGHT'

The blind cat has soft shapes only
to guide it round the cruel familiar room,
radar of memory and probable pain.

Nothing to regret in life finishing,
a good innings in an upper chamber
furnished with care and private nostrils.

You know better, cat. Utter terror
urges your impulsive caravanning,
else where does that cry emerge from?

Do not anthropomorphise me,
says the cat, running on an abrolhos chair
for the twentieth time this evening.

I defy you, cat, I know your mystery.
The cruise from kittendom to chaos
is ending. Love and the murderers arrive.

Kathleen Raine

THE ORACLE IN THE HEART

The oracle in the heart
Spoke last night in deepest dream
One word: 'Regret'; then, thrice attempted,
An utterance more sound than word
But fraught with matter grave
Beyond articulation;
And yet who told must struggle to make known
That truth of the night,
Memory or foreknowledge not to be borne;
But someday must the unendurable all be told.

One other phrase clear among some withdrawn
From memory of the waking mind, or that, like Sibyl's leaves,
Wind-scattered, I failed to gather,
'Your life is trivial', spoken plain. But whose the scorn
Pours on my centuries of days contempt of the immortal world?
Some better life, maybe,

I should or could have lived, and yet
The good and evil I have known and done
In measure as great as heart and mind can hold;
For one poor human life is like another,
Much beauty and much sorrow ours,
And ignorance more; yet, more or less, all tells
Of the one world one story. I have lived
A life, and it suffices, all in all.
It seems the oracle must know
Some other world, some other mode
Of being on the other side of dream
That takes of lives like these
Little account; and yet this world,
Dark to the gods, how bright a paradise
When the heart loves, or when the mind forgets
Memory's load, year by year laid on us,
And welcomes, as if for the first time and for ever, the glad day.

CAMPANULA

This morning, waking
But not yet remembering it was I
Who saw in my window white campanula stars
Against white mistiness
Curving like a shining hill upon the panes,
Remembered or discerned
A way of being those immaculate flowers
Were part of, once, some house
Of elegance and kindness, where I had been,
It seemed, or still remained, until the day
Opened the present and closed
That other time and place the flowers lingered in
A little longer than I. Another decade
It had been, or another life, whose ways
Were fine and clear as these
White visitants from a house of presences forgotten.

Jeremy Reed

FOR AUCTION

A window that never fitted its frame,
a mirror that offered no reflection:
    one seeking a space,
the other a face
to try on: both will break for the wrong one.

A glove with six fingers found on the moor,
a boot that returned each night to a door:
    one seeking a witch,
the other a match,
both for a person with two to make four.

A clock that has stared too long at one wall,
a stag's antler's that stared back in that hall:
    one that would turn back,
the other attack,
possibly bought for a Halloween ball.

A dollshouse that housed a royal midget,
a walking cane that's not ceased to fidget:
    one wishing a dwarf,
one an exorcist,
or paired, a blind imp in a jester's hat.

A stake used to impale a witch's heart,
effigy pins, a grimoire of black art:
    one wanting a crone,
the other poison:
credentials are malice, an extra teat.

Green driftwood salvaged from the winter shore,
a cat that's swifter on three legs than four:
    the one resinous,
the one ominous:
neither will bring warmth to your winter fire.

A white wedding gown, a funeral shroud,
one for passion's heat, and one for death's cold:
    if you're a lady,
acquire both sadly;
if you're a man, then beware of that bride.

Peter Riley

KINGS FIELD

Patches of bare earth on the far hillside: abandoned mines, standing
out like sores through the rough mingling pastoral surface—
scorched by the core of the earth like a passing meteor—sites
of encounter, engagement, victory and defeat, where a piece of
nature split against humanity into metal and slag.

Teeth marks on the shoulder and flank of the hill, scatter of clinker
in the grass, compacted rainwashed mounds glittering with small
surfaces of calcite and quartz . . . The craftsmen of fire
departed, ages ago, decamped and returned home under the sunset
leaving a dying wake of mineral flame—the fire they inhabit,
work in, treading the bright coals, walking the furnaces . . .

Earth substance and sky energy converged at man wedged in the
point of creation—nuclear cocoon—handling the living gold
—fixed screaming to the rock . . .

And in a flash this work is completed and past; we hold the result
in our everyday perceptions, and the whole process, in
retrospect, becomes one moment—the book, closed, becomes
one thing, the coinage fused to a crown,

Leaving us here bewildered, leaving us with a cold in the throat
and a mass of sterile rocks at our feet and no idea what to
connect living to—no continuing occasion or ferial relief—
leaving us holding a medallion against the moon, stamped with
cold royalty.

As if the present is something that already exists.

As if we can pick what we think we want out of the world as a readiness
and let the rest fall aside without getting trapped in a speed
tank of proliferating division, where sympathy is merely the
recourse against a massive dispersal of substance and love strains
against profit to keep a few people together in true lives—we
are outside ourselves; we have no architecture.

It's a dangerous condition, for the world returns us to ourselves in
the formats of our acts in the end—intimately, eventually, the
world has us as we have had the world, right through the boundaries
of our estates the world splits back at us, returns our vocabulary
ground to a knife edge while the residue crumbles and totters over
our heads . . .

As if it were possible to benefit from the treaty of stone and fire as an aftermath, or make or continue anything without inhabiting the generative point, the ecstasy, and bearing its toll. As if our hoarded sentences were anything but paper hedges against the expanse, excuses for lateness and silence, thorn collars for the refusal to say. None of this begins to matter until it is an issue of love.

And we hold on, fingernails tight in the engravure, as the bounty of the original act disperses through the years into cloudy smears of gardenage; nettle, willowherb and bindweed creep up to the very mouth of the mine smothering the work surfaces and smelt holes; smoke and gauze float in the air, blotting the earthscape—

Probably now, as at any other place in history, the trophies, the bright records of humanity, seem to be brought down and strewn abroad in indolence and jealousy, and we call greater and greater threats against ourselves in the failure of satisfaction, bewildered at the lack of personal support, heavy with time resentment, struggling in increasingly blatant hypocrisy to survive on input without living any real event at all—just a few token games, bitter takings without need or purpose. It is the language that fails.

The language lapses, families cooling and drifting apart, bitterly shrugging each other off, emotional victims of pre-failed economics, taking a shabby room in a Victorian terrace to live through the dissolution of the mirror, withdrawal of speech back to the subject—twist of flex in a circlet of yellow plasterwork, old carpet, naked bulb, dusty settee draped in Indian silk—anything, a few bits and pieces, a cold fire. Work discontinued and disproved in the lost kitchen; victims of metallic ambition: experience lived as instant coin.

So there is a void section, a wastage, which can't be reprocessed back to possibility—ice cracks the shell and cups the seed; the faintest reminder of participation floors us. Sense of advance is suspended, 'Purity of heart is to will one thing', and no extant script will recover the retrospective simplicity, the lost whole.

Leave things then for a term aside, attend to the present, the one thing—go shopping, write the letter, disregard recollection ruthlessly adhere to necessity as it stands at any price, be sharp to the very point of trade and trust the climate: alternate freezing and melting we get on the edge of North, water always running down the fields, and the world is exactly what you see.

Sharpened to such an edge, totally engaged into the substance of living, we begin to recall ourselves—how we are truly magnificent at the winning, the gain brought home from distance and obscurity, with always some 'wholeness' behind us, whole because behind us, which the mirror casts back in our faces as marginal loss and we dream from every night. But the only real thing is here in the hand that knows it holds it—life focussed on points of distinction.

To meet this demand there is a flame held back in the eye.

There are points of light all over the valley, where the sun catches car tops, greenhouses and puddles, piercing the winter haze filling the air—a body of light gathering piecemeal towards us, and held there: suspended, animate light between us, that we should be glad to die into, as it throngs up to and over us and soars on the sky horizon.

And how casually we brush it off, with clear excuses, headaches and liabilities, crushing the distance between us to a slight thing—you and I, descend the steps and pass under the cloud into reality, where things also clasp and contain the light, have it in substance, not only shed it—the objects of earth in absolute presence by light or dark holding energy close and ripe, and solid, with nothing to say.

Us, we have a native fire, flame we support in our good will, illumination of the heart page in a cold cell at night, to which all that cosmic display bows: human warmth, that splits the rock and melts out the copper and gold, commingling, consuming us through our bodies . . . that gains as it disperses, consolidates and augments as if flares on the edge of the sky blue lettering of anyone's few, accurate sentences . . . and the more we distribute the more we hold, the more we tell the more we know.

And the sun is safe in the sky and the hills well wrapped in grass and bushes, with outcrops and bare patches here and there where the human construct spat a brief statement to the ground, or bit a chunk from the hillside. The people of the town walk around on a sharp afternoon, struggling to appear through the human casings, formative caustic energy more or less deeply packed in travelling suitcases of flesh and bone, noisily and disruptively breaking out in sparks of meaning while the constant pressure moulds and eats up the active surface—

PL 2 - D

This ferment trapped in us, that belongs somewhere else, outside
our personalised contexts, and is the spirit that moves us
anywhere, forming mere distances into resounding arcades and
terraces, lakes, rings, graveyards . . . and is certainly not at
home in these lumpy sacks, walking bolehills with no proper
site in the world, fighting constantly with shoelaces,
taperecorders and each other in search of a rightful being,
harbouring all the time a perceptive nux that opens to gardens
and edging woods, creates the world, and belongs nowhere.
Even the graves chuck them out.

Human body gurgling and rattling in its excess of language, that stands
between us and the source of life as our only access, sacredly
dithering in the way, between self and its permanent home:
final pivot and moment of peace that must be all body, all
nothing at all.

Don't we already know, and as if in preparation are brought constantly
up against the world of ordinary things, that stand for
personal redundancy—the solid object in its hideous simplicity
that alone gives energy and light any substance or durability,
where language crashes and resurrects, flesh reconstitutes
itself athwart times—it is the message that exceeds us, the
concept not grasped, the emptiness of total being—pure sign
of itself to which such things as metal or poetry or history can
only be another interim script—immoveable and unspeakable,
mournful dump of matter . . .

Go, let the fire through it—don't we immediately and rightly
adore the quick glitter off roadside glass at the sign of
hope? For truth swells in the very moment we live it, holding
round sheer surfaces that cup the soul-fire, burning seed,
candlelight still as standing water beneath its technological
canopy, waiting to lapse into the world—light of a specific
attention kept alive through millennia—simple openness of
response to the authentic script . . .

What if that too, upper sense of the heart furnace, in the end falls,
scatters and dies into featureless geology, what if that too
breaks its perception against the one thing, that nullifies us
and our languages and our preservations, that is the first thing
you see as you enter the portal: the teabag, the feather, the
disused stapler by your arm; friendly local object, not friendly
or local or anything but again the utterly unreachable world-thing,
lying there sucking endeavour towards nonentity . . . Dispersed
stone, unbuyable unmirroring exhibit, terracotta head dripping
with chicken blood and wine—compaction of dust and hair in

the hole at the crossing point of human and terrestrial wills—
the denials and devastations of notions of entirety . . .

Still the authentic light, playing to and from the world, remains
celestial, whether it lasts long or not, still in its torn
jacket this is the new star mounting the rinsed, morning sky,
fresh from the ocean, point of triumph at its own time; that
notifies the successor and warns the sleeper, tracing an arch
across the firmament and finally descending to its dim repose—
the true moment thwarted against great, dreadful extent, and
in response echoing forth the form of a spiritual figure,
full of beauty.

Completely answering the world; and where we leave it, where it
falls, is the talk of the town.

Victoria Rothschild

WATERLOO

On that day the crowd was kneaded together
caked in each other's rust
secretaries mouth hollows to each other
while others swim into the bowl
I, slumped in some shrunken corner,
fish for faces or facts.
A hand is pressed against the glass
pink and white like raspberry fool
and my white face flecks dustily back from someone's blackmac.

On that day the doors peel open
and the cut out paper pattern pieces
unfold onto the platform
I am unseated, unpacked at last.
This tailored maid, pared to bone
handpainted, trims to the surface
scrapes past rot and mould
pruned and cheapened yet
and clears the barriers of glass.

On that day on the cut
my life runs with laughter and tears
the fantasy child of freedom
I imagined in my youth

has grown old into a tramp
fifty quid in my pocket
is just scrumpled paper
no greenbacks now but hounded destitution
it is I that am engraved and castrated.

On that day too a tramp, an old wanderer, picked flowers
and pinned them carefully to his old raggedy coat.
An old lady doubled under her burden—
five full plastic bags and a rucksack—
she would die rather than part from this.
Sirens skin the street
and I find it too dramatic to jump off the bridge
and sit, trying to outstare a cat, on the edge
watching my bleeding feet.
On that day then this dot has an adjunct too
on that day this dot becomes a line
on that day I spent at Waterloo
on that day that day of mine
that day that day
the day they took me away.

Francis Scarfe

TESTAMENT

Let the dead have the books I died my life in,
Stuffing my head with other men's words
Till it is heavy and grey with old ideas.

The old ideas will go with me into the soil
To instruct the worm, until the scholar's skull
Is gouged and clean, and I shall be free.

So you can keep my books, my tongue-tied books,
And chew their poisoned leaves as I did,
Their lotus leaves that steal your wits.

Let them give my hollow clothes to the hollow poor,
The rags in which I hid my life away,
Wool coffins on our incandescent nakedness.

Let them throw away my cash if there's any left.
The best cash I ever had was when I was seven,
A new penny the Mayor threw out of his plumed carriage.

All I would like to have again
Is the fat orange I carried fifty years ago
In the harvest procession through the dusty streets,

I carried it so long it blinded me with its gold,
And even now its memory burns my hand,
A free orange, the only thing I ever owned.

Starry Schor

THE CROWN O' THE EARTH DOTH MELT

i

Time out of mind; remains are more than one can
hope for in an era of decay. Some day we'll lie
elongate, standing on our backs, unless the lava finds us

clinging, sleep-strewn, to the dreams it killed.
Remind me: life is fatal. Chances are
one clear mind in a storm of memory
will heave with wind and burst into the
nothing it has left itself. The

only danger lies in calling home
typhoons. Where does one urge a
haunted thing to rest?
Even in my tiny godless world, I envy women

emptying their lives of ghosts each spring.
At least it leaves them free to
rave at themselves for
trembling in the wake of love,
hallucinating during childbirth.

ii

Does it make a difference to the moon
or terrify another human soul
that half of every maniac is whole;
half of every martyr is a loon?

Many days I let the problem stand
either to forget myself in word-
less ranting or to fall asleep. I heard
they canonized that Eve: give her a hand.

Alan Sillitoe

FISHES

Fishes never change their habits:
A million years seem like a day
As far as fishes' habits go.

Beware of those who change them half as fast
Like people every year or so—
So fast you cannot find a grain
Settled firm in eye or limb.

The constancy of fishes is unique.
They multiply, but keep their habits
In deep and solitary state.

They feel unique and all alone
Not being touched and hardly touching
Even to keep the species spreading—
Unique in never changing habits.

Fishes are flexible and fit the water,
And though continually moving
Never change their habits.

Iain Sinclair

WHERE STEVENSON, SLEEPING

Black covering the green
a body of flies over the flower

not the water that moves
the stones under it, the earth drag

from the bridge; like feathers

&, opposite, the poet's birth-spot
'without a mark, the baby'll die'

only primary sex colours
from machines
that devour finite resources

humankind threaded together
by a fence of electricity

touch the cage & it explodes

C. H. Sisson

THE TIME OF THE YEAR

*

She asks me how I do
It does not matter how
Well and ill are all the same
Now

I live beyond touching
Beyond friendship now
Do not ask oh do not ask
It does not matter how.

**

The night has gone from me
And the day is going
Oh the world oh the world turns
And I on it.

Who, I? Or the world itself
Turning, turning
Between the moon and the clouds
Its head spinning.

***

What price the cul-de-sac
Where you must certainly go?
Patience in getting in
—And the rest you know.

Know it as unknowing
No-way to go, unknown.
The fields whisper to harvest
—You go home.

****

Death, though I cannot go there
Is a neighbouring land

Stretched before my window
But not touched by my hand.

The willows are brown now
It is the time of the year
—Look again, look again, orange!
So have no fear.

Stephen Spender

FROM MY DIARY

'She was', my father said (in an aside),
'A great beauty, forty years ago.'
Out of my crude childhood, I stared at
Our tottering hostess, tremulous
In her armchair, pouring tea from silver—
Her gray silk dress, her violet gaze.
I only saw her being seventy,
I could not see the girl my father saw.

Now that I'm older than my father then was
I go with life-long friends to the same parties
Which we have gone to always.
We seem the same age always
Although the parties sometimes change to funerals
That sometimes used to change to christenings.

Faces we've once loved
Fit into their seven ages as Russian dolls
Into one another. My memory
Penetrates through successive layers
Back to the face which I first saw. So when the last
exterior image is laid under its lid,
Your face first-seen will shine through all.

DOG ROSE
(for KFB)

Dog rose, unfurling
Ruffled petals pink
Afloat on blue air
Through which faint scents blow gold

From pollen which is dust
  Of buried English princes . . .

Once a child tore off
Your small serrated leaves
And twisted their crushed spills
Into his nostrils, filled
His brain with green-juiced briar
Mixed with his sweat. His fists
Hugged the smell of England.

David Sweetman

MEMORIALS

1

This modern centaur is
half machine, half man
with a college forward's
padded shoulders that can
turn him on a dime.

Incestuously, a camera
wheels towards him
and tempted by a silver bone
dangled on a string, he begs
for his war to be done.

I see him whole, in a class
of kids in white, their legs
together with arms flung out—
a class of crosses
lined to a field's limit.

But boys are soon in their anarchy:
a blurr of choppers skimming
over a smoking delta
their throaty ack-ack raging
about the teacher, pleading for order.

2

These wargames lived on.
Through a joint's soft focus
two marines imitated drunks at a party
with a medic waving a plasma bottle
over his prostrate buddy.

Their webbing, stuffed full
of lipsticks, was ready
for the Gook they'd stabbed,
his back a chorus
of rouged mouths, ringent

as the village kids culled
from the confused ossuary
of emaciation: knees like skulls,
chests all fingers and thumbs.
Thus smoke and fantasy could dull

the sound of a magazine snapping
in the breach or the slow
twang of fire. Alone
these could seem innocent, only
the cracking of discarded bones.

3

The childhood monsters lurch
into the shadows
leaving a white-on-white room
where a man learns that a fork
is a lever that can move the earth

and darkness is held back by old movies
that show an enemy clearly marked
with twisted crosses like condemned trees
expecting the axe. His own image shows
death in childish pyjamas and leaves

him confused, yet when he sees a jet pass
an orange duelling scar across the sky he knows:
all violence comes gift-wrapped, its fury
finally boxed and colourful
in The American Century.

Cole Swensen

(Cole is a young American poet who studied calligraphy and bookbinding in London and currently lives in California.)

CAFÉ

(with classical guitar)

music is a clever knife,
it never loses
its way. there are colors
equally untraceable just beyond
the window a storm is growing old,
grey places gold veils
beneath all the streetlights
and walks them off
in a line, quiet from the mist
this
is a storm of tenderness
and this
is the cafe
at the bottom of every cup
of coffee and
rain,
when leading its chained choir
through the streets singing,
is the sole proprietor.

FACE

What in a face speaks the record
that the mouth, word by word
forgets? recognition
rings in blood
it is this, this intraveneous kind of surety
with which your face reoccurs, reoccurs,
it is perfect; I have checked this
and I have watched your hands,
your actions in detail, in dimly lit rooms
your face alone
is visable
it is the only perfection for miles
the opening wing of your face
casts a shadow

and this face has come to haunt me
perhaps I am walking home
past the wharves, it follows.
I have ceased to mind its presence
I strain and try to hear it,
there is a thin sound
coming from the boathouses,
the watchlights almost reach
one another across the shadows.
a movement under the eaves
catches my eye; at a glance
I think it is your face I see
but going closer, no, dozens
of moths are splintering their cocoons,
a fine dust is falling
over everything.

THE DISTANCE

distance falters on these pages
time and silence both
are sealed
and distance falters in these faces
which never move
from what they feel
oh girl, if you could know
your heart like I know
its wheel
or the space between
beyond belief,
there are watermarks upon the ocean
you must hold against
the light to see.

R. S. Thomas

A POET

Disgust tempered by an exquisite
charity, wrapping life's claws
in purest linen—this man
has history to supper,
eats with a supreme tact
from the courses offered to him.

Waiting at table
are the twin graces, patience
and truth; with the candles'
irises in soft clusters
flowering on thin stalks.

Where did he come from?
Pupating against the time
he was needed, he emerged
with wings furled, unrecognised
by the pundits; has spread
them now elegantly
to dazzle: curtains drawn
with a new nonchalance
between barbarism and ourselves.

Patron without condescension
of the art, he teaches flight's
true purpose, which is,
sensitive but not too blinded
by some inner radiance, to be
in delicatest orbit about it.

DEFINITIONS

And this one says:
Poetry is rhyming
word for word. And
this one: Poetry

is that which dies
in translation. It is
the criticism of one
art by another,

Arnold murmurs;
and Coleridge: Order
beyond order. And
you, I ask, looking

at myself towards
life's end in a pitiless
mirror, What do you
say poetry is? No

answer. Teeth must remain
clenched on the sparerib
of language I have rasped
at fifty odd years.

Hugo Williams

THE RIBBON

I thought she'd taken all her things
but I was wrong. Wherever I go
I catch glimpses of my damnation.

Is that too strong a word? You wouldn't think so
if you could see this lovely ribbon
wound around my hand.

Don't tell me, I know,
I'm mumbling to myself again. I'm like King Kong
picking among the ruins of New York
for a clue to his malady.

I wonder what they were like,
these odds and ends,
collecting dust, though freed at last from blame.
Did they look the same
when she held them in her hand?

It seems ridiculous
how everything here acknowledges her touch,
including me, including this tangled ribbon.

Perhaps you were right after all
and I make too much of it. I'll just sit here now
and try to undo these knots—
I'll be with you in a minute, if you can wait.

POINTS OF VIEW

DURRELL

LAWRENCE DURRELL: *Collected Poems 1931–1974*, edited by James A. Brigham (Faber and Faber, London £9·00)

Lawrence Durrell must be sixty-nine years old. His first book of poems from Faber, was *A Private Country* (1943), and the second was *Cities, Plains and People* (1946). Durrell was thirty-four by then, and it is small wonder that to my own later generation he seemed to have sprung from nowhere, perfectly mature, knowing the world and fully armed with his qualities. But he was born in 1912, and his first poem was at least privately published in 1931 when he was nineteen. That is what you might expect. His sudden appearance of full maturity in 1943 was a matter of justified self-censorship. Now for the first time we have the truly complete poems down to 1974, including nearly every poem ever printed, with dates added and dedications and notes restored.

Picking one's way through Durrell's poetry, we might notice one or two things. The very early Durrell, from the period of Paris and Corfu, is already hard to mistake for anyone else. But until 1938 he was no more than talented. He was a poet of spring rain and youthful love. There were touches of Rupert Brooke about his verse style, and he had learnt almost nothing then from Eliot, Pound or Empson. These early poems have merit and they were well worth rescuing, but their chief value is to show how long, and how personal, was his struggle for style. Although I am nineteen years younger, a conservative provincial schooling put me as a young man into similar difficulties. It is hard to have much sympathy today with that view of the modern tradition in English poetry which steps from Hardy and the Georgians straight to Larkin and Betjeman, as if Pound and Eliot and David Jones had never written. But there were and still are alternative traditions to American or French modernism, and other styles, which poets fought with their life-blood to hammer out. Durrell has been a highly original poet, he has invented his style. He has no obvious ancestors or successors. He is not a natural poet like D. H. Lawrence, who hardly went beyond what he could do perfectly by instinct. He is a personal, unique poet in the same sense as Yeats, and his best poems are the reward and the fruit of many years of work.

Another observation of the same kind arises from this full publication. It lacks, thank heaven, a mortuary completeness, stopping in 1974, so that I could calculate another volume may be due soon. But it does make it quite clear that the Muses have not deserted Durrell. The poem *Seferis*, on the death of his old friend (1972) is as moving and as beautiful in its way as anything he has ever written, or that anyone else has written in the last ten years. It is full and laconic at the same time, as the sea is. In another vein, some of his poems have always been *boutades*, almost too witty to be poems. As he has grown older he has become a sage, but he continued as witty as ever through the early seventies, and the wit is still disturbingly youthful. Some of the images, like the wit, are so sharp that printed together in a collection they fight against one another; it is a mistake to read too many at once. I made that mistake with the old collected Durrell when it came out in 1968, and suffered a revulsion. Was it Auden who said it was bad manners to be brilliant absolutely all the time? But taken one by one these lines, and these poems, are stinging, strong and admirable. They go deeper into the matter of poetry than any one else's brilliant lines or poems.

I am not sure where or how Lawrence Durrell found his voice, but the experience of Greece and the poetry of George Seferis surely had something to do with it. Still, it is hardly deniable that *The Death of General Uncebunke* (1938), a supremely English subject treated with intimate compassion and irony, was his first great poem. It was another England, of course, in those days and Durrell was brought up as a boy in British India. The first Greek poem, *Carol on Corfu*, is hardly Greek at all, but almost purely Shakespearean. Durrell in fact is the only poet of his generation who could have held his own in the company and in the verse of *Love's Labour's Lost.*

In a lecture about the Romans of the Augustan age, the late Eduard Fraenkel once remarked that the deeper a man was then, the deeper Greece entered into him. Of those into whom Greece entered at all in Durrell's generation, the same saying seems to be mysteriously true. But in his case it was not just the idyllic Greece, the peaceful, pre-war countryside. As late as 1939 he was an intellectual with roots in Paris as well as Greece. The poem on *Father Nicholas, His Death: Corfu* (1939) does belong to that idyllic Greece, but it has a good deal in common with Uncebunke. At about the same period, in a sermon from a verse play, now reprinted for the first time, one can spot the first undeniable influence of Eliot. The Greek poems begin to come thick and fast under the shadow of European war, in 1940, and in the dark days of defeat.

It may be worth saying that Durrell has never been a political poet, less so for example even than George Seferis. Those who prefer some salt of commitment and some pepper of Greek politics with their poetry will have to find a poet elsewhere. How honourably Durrell lived through these years, and the deadly period that followed them, we know from his writings in prose. It is important not to confuse that with his poetry. In poems his persona more frequently resembles that of a Chinese lover in one of Arthur Waley's translations. It is true, I suppose, that most of history is what is done to us, not what we do. Even in his saddest poems about Cyprus, his work is like Prospero's, to exorcise the evil, to calm it away with music. If you did not know already what those Cyprus poems were about, you would very possibly miss the intensity of their bitterness.

Somewhere in Lawrence Durrell's soul is a hermit, and I believe it was the hermit, not a prophet or a man of action, who ripened through so many poems into wisdom. The hermit was fully grown by 1940 and he haunts a longish poem that comes close to greatness, the biography of Fangbrand, written then in Mykonos when it was, as they say, unspoilt. One might almost feel that in this poem Durrell foresaw his own future, though wrongly as things turned out. 'I want', he writes in a note to *Conon in Exile*, 'my total poetic work to add up as a kind of tapestry of people, some real, some imaginary.' That note, reprinted now for the first time since 1943, has always been an apparent truth about the poems of this period. Conon, we are also told, is a mask for the poet himself. *Conon in Exile* therefore, is part of the long and sad meditation on the writer as hermit and the writer as lover, which reaches a sort of conclusion in the splendid verses *On First Looking into Loeb's Horace* (1943).

The same material was used later in the Alexandria Quartet, though I personally far prefer it in its pure and brief form in the poems about Fangbrand and Conon and Horace. The Horace poem in particular is remarkable. It is written simply and lucidly, with masterly authority, in a loose, quite original stanza form which is effective and unexpected at every reading.

It is as true about Horace as his *Bryon* is about Bryon. Like the Bryon poem, again it is long enough to say a good deal yet it has a pared quality, a clarity of progression, which is admirable. It surely comes close to the core of Lawrence Durrell's poetry. But it by no means exhausts the categories. It is only two poems away from *A Ballad of the Good Lord Nelson*, still in 1943. Then he was thirty-two. The decision of Faber's to print his first book in that difficult year must have been taken by T. S. Eliot himself. A poem dedicated to Eliot appears in 1945. Some earlier honours are due to the Fortune Press, who included some Durrell in a collection called *Proems* in 1938. I note that only because the present editor does not mention it; publishers of poetry deserve what few compliments they get.

Durrell has always been famous for pure lyrics, but his strength has often been in the rather long lyric and the sequence. It is not only their scale that singles out *Uncebunke* at the end of the thirties, and *Cities, Plains and People* in 1946, but within the possibilities, the agreed limits of modern lyric poetry, their scale is remarkable. *Deus Loci* was still to come (1950), and perfect short lyrics like *Lesbos* (1953) and others as recently written as the seventies; yet nothing written since the year after the war has matched the scale and the range of *Cities, Plains and People*.

Cities, Plains and People conveys a sense of range which analysis will not disappoint. I would not like to have to state concisely what it says or does, but I take it was a poem of autobiography and at the same time a *tour d'horizon* of what the world is like, what an intellectual and what a poet shall make of it. The first poems are tentative and thrilling. The last one, which I have known by heart since soon after it was first printed, has an intoxicating charm and, in its second stanza, a Shakespearean inevitability It is hard to confront Shakespeare's ghost head-on in modern poetry. Lawrence Durrell has dealt with that sinewy phantom with complete grace and simplicity. Among other things, he has never ceased to be a superb phrase-maker. Memorable line follows memorable line throughout these poems. I had forgotten, until this rereading, the poets who could only found 'Pulpits of smoke like Blake's Jerusalem', and Bede who softly 'Blew out desire and went to bed'. Among these stanzas are to be found a premonition of *Deus Loci*, an annotated *Corfu*, many doom-laden lines about Europe, and the splendid twelve lines about the yellow Emperor who visits us in Lawrence or in Blake.

Now darkness comes to Europe
Dedicated by a soft unearthly jazz.
The greater hearts contract their joys
By silence to the very gem,
While the impertinent reformers,
Barbarians with secretaries move,
Whom old Cavafy pictured,
Whom no war can remove.

It is hard to choose one verse of a few lines and to reject others. I have not in general quoted much of the poetry of Lawrence Durrell here because I think it unnecessary to quote famous poems that are in fact probably familiar to most readers. But if this collection should be read by someone who has it all before him, how I do envy that person. To have written a dozen or two dozen perfect lyrices is an extremely rare achievement. To have a new poet in front of you who has done that in your own lifetime or in living memory is a comparably rare pleasure. And yet, Durrell has never been praised and admired quite as much as he deserved. He is always being 'revived' as if he were not strong. Why is he not heaped with honours? Why will he not get the Nobel Prize? Because tourism overtook Greece? Because of the Alexandria Quartet? Something to do with sex? Snobbery or envy? Because he simply gives pleasure? Or because of his autodidactic opinions? But all poets are autodidacts (e.g. Eliot) and most would like to give more pleasure than they do. And here is a man whose whole life has been devoted headlong to poetry, who is almost certainly a great poet—by which I mean great whether you like it or not. Permanent. It stays on the page. It stands up. When you have finished with Durrell he is still there. A poet of certain experiences, yes. Limited, yes. But all the same, surely, a great poet in our time, and what recognition have we given him?

Of course this question is right outside the poetry, and yet a thread leads from it into certain poems. It has something to do with wide symbolic range which can be mistaken for imprecision or vagueness, with the number of sweet tastes or tones and the number of appealing images which are bearable in poems, with that which seems to say Give up or Why fight it, rather than Strive, Suffer, Endure. It has surely something to do with sex. What an irony in that case that Lawrence Durrell has dealt fully and clearly with the syndrome of puritan criticism of this kind. If I am wrong about the lack of acknowledgement or about the root cause of it, then it still remains to be explained. I am not speaking of the higher literary criticism, which is as sudden as God and beyond explanation of any kind, but only of some grudging attitudes to Durrell's work that I have encountered, never from anyone I respected.

But between 1938 and 1948, or by argument from similar examples between 1938 and 1958, he was a genius of a kind, an indispensable poet. By then the Cyprus poems had been written but, as we have seen, it is still mere ignorance to suppose that at that time, at the age of forty-six, Durrell went to sleep.

> I shall die one day I suppose
> In this old Turkish house I inhabit:
> A ragged banana-leaf outside and here
> On the sill in a jam-jar a rock rose.

The relaxed musical surface of lyric poems depends as much today as it did in the fifteen nineties on vigour, on the abundance of life. Usually the perogative of youth, today's cowed youth picks its way overcarefully through critical minefields, and lyric poetry is left to the perpetual youthfulness of poets like Durrell. Maybe the key to his ability is in his ear. How quantitative his sad or serious lyrics are. How little stress rhythm they allow. How gently they syncopate. In boisterous moods he writes in quite another manner. Where did Durrell learn his slow, convincing lyric tones? I am grateful that today there are no metrical scholars at all capable of analysing his lovely performance. But the interesting question remains, whether the definition of lyric poetry might be metrical after all.

PETER LEVI

Lawrence Durrell and Alfred Perles in Chelsea.

ON THE THRESHOLD OF LANGUAGE

W. S. GRAHAM: *Collected Poems 1942–1977* (Faber and Faber, London £9)

When the cry went up that poetry was barbaric, impossible even after the holocaust, I presume it was the so-called 'poetical' treatment of things, and the 'aesthetically pleasing' which seemed particularly offensive. Pascal's description 'poète et non honnête homme' was to be taken seriously, became indeed a matter of grave importance. Dishonesty had become, still is, intolerable in the face of the evidence. And that is why the greatest poetry being written now is profoundly honest, painfully self-scrutinising. Geoffrey Hill has expressed what others would echo when talking about one of his poems: 'But I want the poem to have this dubious end; because I feel dubious; and the whole business is dubious.' And out of this doubt has come a surgeon for the language in the shape of W. S. Graham. Born in Scotland in 1918, his work bears consistent evidence of a profound distrust of language, reads like a testament of doubt; but he is an apostle for accurate language, and his ambition, like others before him, to purify the dialect by stripping his poems right down, emptying them of complications like proper names, dissecting the poetic process and laying open the anatomy of the poem even as he writes it. Language, and more particularly the language of poetry is, at bottom, Graham's only 'subject'. He takes to its conclusion Stevens' dry statement: 'Poetry is the subject of the poem,/From this the poem comes and/To this returns.' But how wittily and how unsettlingly Graham demonstrates the point! We the gentle and well-trained readers, on the lookout for such devices as personae and 'shifting tone' are still brought up with a jolt when our poet admits 'I am only out here to walk or/Make this poem up.' Graham scours his own and the reader's assumptions and expectations. Here are the third and fourth stanzas of 'What is the Language Using Us For?' from his book *Implements in their Places*, 1977.

> Let us observe Malcolm Mooney.
>
> Let us get through the suburbs and drive
> Out further just for fun to see
> What he will do. Reader, it does
> Not matter. He is only going to be
>
> Myself and for you slightly you
> Wanting to be another. He fell
> He falls (Tenses are everywhere.)
> Deep down into a glass jail.

The usual syntactic rules are broken but the sense remains intact. The dissection is going on before our eyes; it is more important, or at least equally important, that (Tenses are everywhere.), so the statement is no mere parenthesis but a sentence which in a conventional syntax would be disruptive. For Graham, the 'narrative' is only a structure there to be disrupted; a poem that ran on without comment or disruption must be a thing of great suspicion. There is some deception at work in the 'apparently artless', some cover-up which Graham will not allow. Any manipulation of the reader is not to be carried on more or less insidiously (as in Browning) but openly, even to the extent of making it the subject of the poem. The brackets here do not so much, in Christopher Ricks's phrase 'establish a co-existing zone', as remind us there is only the one shifting zone of language which we are all perforce on, the moment we use it. The parenthesis is just to remind us, in case we have forgotten, that the language is using us and not vice-versa. As a writer, Graham has to suffer the recurrent confrontation with his 'frightening abstract/Table of silence' from which language appears a monstrous mass which 'swings away' when he tries to use it. Writing is an exceedingly tricky business and of necessity self-conscious. No image is allowed to pass unchallenged; here is the end of *Dear Bryan Wynter*:

> I know I make a symbol
> Of the foxglove on the wall.
> It is because it knows you.

It might seem that such insistent self-scrutiny and running commentary would end by evacuating the poem of all significance and collapse it into itself. In less capable hands (and it is a common enough practice now to write about writing) this would surely happen; but Graham triumphs not only because he has the daring to go further than anyone else, but also because the words he does admit have a concrete resilience, his repeated phrases a peculiar resonance. Even as I say this I am conscious that in one of the most revolutionary and outrageous poems *Enter a Cloud* Graham even circumscribes the words he has chosen, admitting in the last section, very wittily, that he chose them precisely for the reason that they were 'hard'. In this poem Graham is lying on Zennor Hill (so often mentioned that we and the poet may become convinced of its reality as solid ground), and as precisely as possible attempts to 'write the cloud' as it passes over without being metaphorical or poetical about it but geographical and factual instead:

> Between Zennor and Gurnard's
> Head, an elongated
> White anvil is sailing
> Not wanting to be a symbol.

By section 5 the cloud has disappeared and it is time to collapse the poem:

> Thank you. And for your applause.
> It has been a pleasure. I
> Have never enjoyed speaking more.
> May I also thank the real ones
> Who have made this possible.
> First the cloud itself. And now
> Gurnard's Head and Zennor
> Head. . . . . .
> And good words like brambles,
> Bower, spiked, fox, anvil, teeling.

The magician explains his conjuring trick and takes a bow (denying himself thereby any real sense of self-congratulation from the poem). It is the end result of poetry seen as a rigorous game. As someone said of that vast anatomy of *Kubla Khan*, *The Road to Xanadu*, it is the sort of thing to be done once and never again!

Good words; Graham's major poems (*The White Threshold*, *The Nightfishing*, *The Dark Dialogues*), are full of them. Many are applied to that 'fond metaphor the sea'. The speaking, mingling, welcome-roaring and continual sea. And what better metaphor for a language that fluctuates and 'swings away'? The effect of reading these longer poems is like being spellbound for as long as they last, and for some time after. They unwind like sinuous paths that have to be followed in the dark; they exist against the pressing silence that threatens the poem at every turn. The first section of *The Nightfishing*, from the book of that name (1955), is one of Graham's masterly achievements. He manages to give extraordinary, I might say magical weight to his short lines, without ever falling into portentousness:

> Very gently struck
> The quay night bell.
>
> Now within the dead
> Of night and the dead

Of my life I hear
My name called from far out.

He achieves with that heavy repetition of 'dead' something of Donne's gravity in his line 'Tis the yeares midnight, and it is the dayes', that begins his *Nocturnall upon S. Lucies day*. Graham the man is now in the middle way and speaks from the dead of his life, in the darkness and at the nadir. It is a compelling moment, one of spellbound suspension between melting and freezing. The first two lines sound the bell; we hear a 'pause of silence' in the white space while the sound of the bell travels down into the poet's silence where it will find an echo. The voice continues:

I'm come to this place
(Come to this place)
Which I'll not pass
Though one shall pass
Wearing seemingly
This look I move as.

We are reminded of Eliot's '(Come in under the shadow of this red rock)', though with Graham it is even less sure how we should '(Come to this place)', and more uncertain what we shall find there. Graham himself is unsure because language is changing his own identity (or limiting it), as he uses it. In later poems it is Malcolm Mooney who we meet. For Graham, Eliot's phrase 'the poetry does not matter' can scarcely have meaning since all this poet's struggles exist on the threshold of language itself and can have no appeal to some faith beyond that language. And George Steiner's opinion the 'the ineffable lies beyond the frontiers of the word' finds a response in Graham's equal insistence on the importance of saying (in a passage that is one of the most affirming, for he is finally a poet of affirmation):

I speak across the vast
Dialogues in which we go
To clench my words against
Time or the lack of time
Hoping that for a moment
They will become for me
A place I can think in,
And think anything in,
An aside from the monstrous.

He must do this 'Because always language/Is where the people are.' The language is precious because with it we can, perhaps, break out of silent isolation. I am quoting from *The Dark Dialogues*, a poem in Graham's collection *Malcolm Mooney's Land*, 1970. I want to discuss this poem in more detail because it shares much with the other long poems and provides an interesting comparison with Coleridge's *Frost at Midnight*, prompted by Graham himself:

Wheesht, children, and sleep
As I break the raker up,
It is only the stranger
Hissing in the grate.

Like Coleridge before him, Graham is sitting up late by the fire and enters into a meditation that embraces the present and the past of his childhood. In Graham's case it also involves different voices, one of them that of the children's mother, but the distinctions between them are not drawn sharp enough to be more than of negligible importance. Coleridge's concrete imagination, aided by memory, helps him to avoid slipping back into his usual 'abstruser musings', thoughts which in an earlier poem were dubbed 'unregenerate'; the resulting poem is a verbal triumph and gives, in Humphry House's phrase, 'an extraordinary sense of the mind's very being' (and a mind in wonderful control of its ordering consciousness, believing sufficiently in the efficacy of language to convey its vision of order). Such a belief, rooted in the idea that language can finally take care of itself when the passion to express a truth is strong enough, enables Coleridge to write his magnificent ending, addressed to the sleeping Hartley, concerning the nature of God. And now we hear Graham, in a darker phase:

Believe me I would ask
Forgiveness but who
Would I ask forgiveness from?

So he is thrown once again on to his own resources; he must somehow construct for himself a place to live in, 'an aside from the monstrous', and he can only do this with words. In *the mother's voice* (section 2) the recourse to using words is not open; the psyche is not reassured by the sleeping children as Coleridge's was. Rather, a chill and baffling alienation sets in:

And I hear them breathe and turn
Over in their sleep
As I sit here becoming
Hardly who I know.

The tenderness towards the children seems to express itself in a concern to protect them from the overwhelming isolation and fluctuation of adulthood. This voice does not resolve, but changes in the third section to the father's voice, more immediately identifiable as Grahams' own. His only existence is by making the words of the poem as he writes it occur. He speaks in his despair:

Here I am makeshift made
By artifice to fall
Upon a makeshift time.

The only effect evoking his childhood seems to have is of bringing the present into starker relief:

Otherwise I go
Only as a shell
Of my former self.

The poem becomes increasingly tortuous, and threatens to collapse back into darkness; but the poet survives this terrible confrontation in the dead of night and passes beyond it. What might have been an empty gesture, a shadow play performed in a vacuum, is transformed for the poet into an act of faith and love. If Eliot returns to know the place for the first time, Graham finds a kind of redemption in the poem itself, with all its questioning and repetition. He is indeed undefeated because he has gone on trying, wrestling with approximate speech. It has been no less than his life's task, and at the end of *The Dark Dialogues* we have the privilege of glimpsing the reward of this effort. The words he uses finally afford him a place to think in (the word 'word' is secure enough, being perfectly descriptive of itself). Exquisitely, at the end, he breaks the monotonous and trapping circle of self, looks up from his writing table and witnesses a real event, which transforms inside him, as though for an instant he has reached his favourite place on the 'other side of language':

There is no other place
Than where I am, between
This word and the next.
Maybe I should expect
To find myself only
Saying that again
Here now at the end.
Yet over the great
Gantries and cantilevers

Of love, a sky, real and
Particular is slowly
Startled into light.

STEPHEN ROMER

DAVID JONES: MAKER OF SIGNS

DAVID JONES: *The Roman Quarry and other sequences*, edited by Harman Grisewood and René Hague (Agenda Editions £7·50)
NICOLETE GRAY: *The Painted Inscriptions of David Jones* (Gordon Fraser £29·50)
WILLIAM BLISSET: *The Long Conversation—A Memoir of David Jones* (Oxford University Press £9·75)

1981 has turned out to be a remarkable year for celebration of the memory of David Jones: in the summer the Tate Gallery mounted a splendid and satisfying exhibition of his drawings, engravings and inscriptions, which went subsequently to Sheffield and Cardiff; versions for radio of *In Parenthesis* and *The Sleeping Lord* were broadcast by the BBC; the David Jones Society, founded at Aberystwyth in 1975, continues to flourish in its seventh year (the admirable David Blamires, who edits the society's newsletter from Manchester University, announced in its twenty-ninth number that 'activity continues unabated on the David Jones front'); a number of his works came up for sale at Sotheby's in November; and three books, prepared for the presses by four of his close friends, provide further evidence (if, indeed, such evidence is still required) that it is not improper to speak of David Jones in the same breath as Joyce, Pound and Eliot. Seven years after his death, David Jones is coming to that widespread recognition which his gifts as writer and visual artist surely deserve.

Sadly, it must also be noted that 1981 deprived us of probably the ablest and most perceptive of commentators on the writings of David Jones. René Hague, who died in Ireland last January, was a man of formidable learning, lightly worn, and of extraordinary energy, a large part of which he devoted to guiding the reader through the intricacies and difficulties of his friend's writings. Hague's commentary on *The Anathemata* (Christopher Skelton, 1977) is a masterpiece of its kind, a model for such exegetical studies, and his assembly (with Harman Grisewood) of David Jones's unpublished manuscripts into the text of *The Roman Quarry* stands as a proper memorial to a very remarkable man, who is sorely missed by his friends. René Hague and Harman Grisewood were presented with a formidable task, in the shape of some 1,300 sheets of handwritten foolscap, which represented, in part, 'a large-scale epic poem with prose interludes' of which the published fragments, *The Anathemata* and *The Sleeping Lord*, were but a part. Five years at hard labour enabled the editors to make from that primordial chaos something which, if not in the shape which David Jones would have intended had he been able to complete his design, nevertheless affirmed their belief that 'all of David's creative writing should be available'.

The Roman Quarry, as one would expect, is not patient of rapid assimilation: there are alternative versions of passages which appear in the published works; there is a mass of new material; and from the text we now have, there shine those bright and intricate images so characteristic of David Jones at his best.

And on the heights above the spume-fret
the albescent chalk
cliffs gleam-bright

her sea-ward parapets.
    It was, he said, as though the White Island
lay at anchor
    riding a mooring
just off Europa's main.
And had so lain
    for countless millennia back
and would so lie
    hodiern, modern, sempitern.

(*The Narrows*)

I can recall my own excitement when David Jones first read to me the draft incorporating the lines quoted above. It was around that time that he would, in his then enfeebled state of health, confined to the care of the Little Company of Mary at Calvary Nursing Home in Harrow, give vent to his frustration: 'There's still so much I have to do!' Some of us cherished the hope that he might yet, by a supreme effort, achieve the completion of that huge work which had been in his mind constantly since his visit to Palestine, and Jerusalem in particular, in 1934. That hope is now extinguished, but those who care for the things David was trying to do in all his creative works, who feel some sense of affinity with that world of *anamnesis* so central to all his conceptions, will acknowledge their debt of gratitude to René Hague and Harman Grisewood (and to William Cookson, the publisher), for making available the material, however rawly it may appear, contained in *The Roman Quarry*.

Nicolete Gray's book, *The Painted Inscriptions of David Jones*, is sheer delight to those who rejoice in the wonderfully expressive textures of David Jones's pieces of lettering. It is also an expensive volume (just short of thirty pounds), and there may be those who will complain that not all of the illustrations are in colour, since colour was an integral part of the artist's expressive technique in this medium. These inscriptions make the link between the writings and the drawings of David Jones: they *illuminate*, as did manuscripts of an earlier age, liturgical texts, poetical quotations from such diverse sources as Ovid, Virgil, Thomas Aquinas, Chaucer, Malory, Dunbar, Tennyson, Joyce, Welsh poems and proverbs, the Gospels and the Psalms—a fair indication of the catholic range of David Jones's reading.

The point, so cogently made by Nicolete Gray in her introduction, is that these inscriptions are true works of art, to be enjoyed for their visual, as well as their literal content. What they are doing, as David Jones explains in a letter to Nicolete Gray in 1961, is to explore the 'feeling for the evocative nature of words as expressed in shapes'. This book is a sure source of pleasure for those who are able to recognize in David Jones a most eminent exponent of the art of lettering. William Blissett's memoir, *The Long Conversation*, is altogether a slighter work than the two volumes mentioned above, but not the less entertaining for that. It is a carefully detailed record of Professor Blissett's visits to David Jones between 1959 and 1974, first at Northwick Lodge on Harrow Hill, then at Monksdene Residential Hotel, and finally Calvary Nursing Home on Sudbury Hill where David Jones spent his remaining years after a fall and a stroke in 1970. As René Hague pointed out, David Jones had the gift of being able to share laughter with his friends, and Blissett's account includes much reminiscence of mirth and delight. He prints a letter from the Canadian poet and translator, George Johnston, which catches exactly the picture of David Jones as we knew him in those last years, confined to quarters in the nursing home, eating meals from a tray.

He had a hard time hoisting himself up in bed, but he talks on, not a monologue by any means, we are both in on it, but he did most of the talking. He began to load up his fork; it was as slow as possible & almost numb & yet in effect precise, but he would get a bit of egg on & then try to think of a word & put his hand to his eyes & then apparently drift off & absent-mindedly put a bit of tomato on too & then he would think of the word & the talk would come to a focus again, but the knife and fork get laid down & he picks up the tea & brings it almost to his mouth but it didn't get there & instead got put back on the saucer again & then back to the fork: more egg, a bit of ham, tomato, it is now a heroic forkful but it will get cut down again & re-shaped before it at last gets carried to his mouth. He gave the impression of not knowing the knife and fork were there but it was all beautifully done just the same.

The Long Conversation gives the reader exactly what its title promises. The book is an affectionate and highly entertaining tribute from a friend of many years' standing.

David Jones was born on All Saints' Day, 1 November, 1895, and he died in 1974, on Monday 28 October, just a few days before what would have been his seventy-ninth birthday. His writings are conveniently assembled in just half a dozen volumes: *In Parenthesis* (1937), *The Anathemata* (1952), *The Sleeping Lord* (1974), *The Roman Quarry* (1981), and the two books of prose pieces, edited by Harman Grisewood, *Epoch and Artist* (1959) and *The Dying Gaul* (1978). Through careful and thorough study of this *oeuvre*, aided by the wealth of critical and biographical apparatus which has accumulated over the years, I believe we are coming to see what is the rightful place allocated to David Jones in the annals of twentieth-century literature. René Hague has succeeded in clearing away many of the obstacles to a real appreciation of *The Anathemata*, and Christine Pagnoulle's thesis (as yet, unpublished) will perform a similar service for readers of the fragments contained in *The Sleeping Lord*. There is time yet for a full-scale biography to follow *Dai Greatcoat* (1980), the self-portrait in his letters, put together by René Hague. At last, I believe, we are in a position to take stock of David Jones's achievements in literature and in the visual arts; it is no longer possible to regard him as some kind of 'cult figure'—a favourite term of dismissal with some would-be critics.

I have the comfortable feeling that the year now behind us has seen much which will serve to enhance the reputation of David Jones, and to bring his work to the notice of a significantly wider readership than hitherto. David Jones was, perhaps, the most remarkable man I have met: a truly serious artist (and, I believe, a great one in several ways), and a most amusing, delightful and sociable human being. Tom Burns, in an obituary notice in *The Tablet*, said that he was, quite simply, 'a holy man'. He rejoiced in his Welsh ancestry, he maintained a steadfast adherence to the Catholic faith which he adopted in 1921, he had a real and lasting devotion to the things of this island of Britain, and he created, as William Blake had done before him, works of literature and art which were of profound significance. David Jones was, in fact, a maker of signs—though it is not easy to set down in simple terms all the implications which that brief description, 'a maker of signs', carries with it. As David Jones himself wrote:

The artist deals wholly in signs. His signs must be valid, that is, valid for him and, normally, for the culture that has made him.

PETER ORR

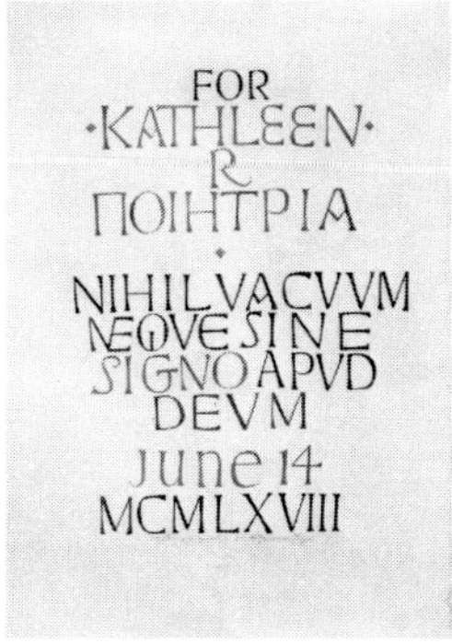

For Kathleen (*Raine*). This seems to be the last inscription made by David Jones.

GASCOYNE'S CHOICE

JEREMY REED: *Bleecker Street* (Carcanet New Press £2·95)

If I had never heard of Jeremy Reed before, I feel sure I should nevertheless have at once recognized in this book a distinctive new voice. But Jeremy Reed's work has appeared widely in magazines and from the small presses, and I have read several of his shorter previous little-press edition books already (including notably 'Saints and Psychotics', published by Alan Clodd of Enitharmon).

It is unfortunately impossible in a brief review to convey an adequate idea of the richness of imaginative range and the maturity of technical control manifested in this book, which Jeremy Reed himself, incidentally, considers to be in most ways his first. But to give some idea of the kind of subject-matter, one needs to begin by explaining the choice of this collection's title, for the benefit of such readers as might conceivably suppose Bleecker Street to be one of those innumerable locales that have had a 'blues number' named after them. In fact, the volume is prefaced by a couple of brief quotations, one from Webster, the first from Hart Crane (extracted from a poem called *Possessions*):

> And I, entering, take up the stone
> As quiet as you can make a man . . .
> In Bleecker Street, still trenchant in a void.

Here we have an immediate clue to one of Jeremy Reed's most enduring obsessions, or rather one of the principal figures in the kind of personal mythology he has built up for himself and upon which his imaginative vision is most often to be found centered.

With Hart Crane, the homosexual boozer who wrote himself dry, to describe him in coarse journalistic terms, and who finally flung himself into the Atlantic on a return voyage from Florida to New York—an American *poete maudit* if ever there was one, and one of the few 20th Century American poets who can reasonably be categorized as 'visionary'—is now inseparably linked the name of Samuel Greenburg, a sort of consumptive New York Chatterton if one thinks of him in terms of legend, but rather a Rimbaud who died in hospital (aged twenty-three) like the latter, rather than in an attic. If one takes his startling originality into account, the quality in his fragmentary manuscript remains qualified as 'unspeakably eerie' by Crane, who had no hesitation in adopting many images, phrases and turns of diction from the unknown dead boy and thus in a way immortalizing him without being aware of doing so. And it is astonishing to think that one of Jeremy Reed's earlier sequences, *The Isthmus of Samuel Greenburg*, though published in 1976, was actually written three years before that date, and already shows a singular originality and a distinct style very much his own.

The back-cover note to *Bleeker Street* says that Jeremy Reed has been called a 'latter day Jacobean', which, however misleading such labels may sometimes turn out to be, does seem to me in this instance to have considerable justification, not simply because he is 'much possessed by death', as who is not, but because of his obvious feeling of affinity with that still possibly underestimated but certainly extraordinary phenomenon, Thomas Beddoes, for some time referred to, if at all, as 'the last Jacobean'. It may not be altogether irrelevant to recall in this connection that at the time when I first began occasionally to encounter Dylan Thomas, I became aware that he had been possessed since his early 'teens with a passionate enthusiasm for Beddoes and that he and our mutual friend Norman Cameron had a long-term, never-to-be fulfilled ambition to reduce the vast and untidy *Death's Jest Book* to stageable proportions. I cannot refrain from observing, before leaving this aspect of Mr. Reed's poetic character, that Djuna Barnes—to whom *Toque*, which I consider to be one of the most outstandingly remarkable items in this collection, is dedicated—is the author of that unique (and mutilated, were it but known) masterpiece *Nightwood*, the gorgeously baroque prose of which is resonant with Jacobean undertones and reverberations.

It might be said here that it is debatable whether the *expression* of emotion is in fact a function proper to specifically contemporary poetry, though as I've said before it is impossible to conceive of a born poet who was not gifted with unusual sensibility and hence liable to experience the basic human emotions with a perhaps heightened intensity, and also to be moved by certain things that the so-called normal man does not have the capacity or at any rate the inclination to notice or react to. But insofar as Jeremy Reed's poems convey an indication of the emotions felt in relation to the subject-matter, which the spokesmen of characteristically *modern* poetry have declared to be of secondary importance ('A poem should not mean but be' might be the ruling maxim of a large number of French and continental poets as well as of many Americans), then I do not think it misleading to describe them as predominantly bleak in feeling, sometimes suggesting a precarious balance on the verge of despair held back only by a furious desire to continue creating poetry of ever-increasing insight and formal control. The degree of development of the latter which he has already achieved is strikingly demonstrated in such a poem as *Marlowe's Letter to Thomas Walsingham* in the present collection.

Finally, it should be remarked that in Jeremy Reed's poetry the provincial narrowness of outlook and awareness that made so much of the British poetic output of a decade or two ago appear so dull and limited in aim, when compared with what was being written elsewhere in the world, is conspicuously absent. By way of bringing this article to a conclusion, I should like to quote the second of the two stanzas which constitute the poem entitled *Elegy-Europe*, as the lines seem to illustrate so well the kind of qualities that this poet possesses:

I show you my fingers; how they are bald
with tracings over paper for the one
poem that's concealed on the other side
of language, not the Wall. We're dressed in white,
but invisible to the underground.
Your fatigue would demand a hotel but
we're never sure of what is composite
or who. Nor why the key-holes are stained red.

DAVID GASCOYNE

GRAVE WEIGHT, AND THE SINGING VOICE

C. H. SISSON: *Exactions*, SBN 85635 332 9 (Carcanet New Press Ltd. Paperback £2·95p)
SIMON LOWY: *Melusine & the Nigredo*, SBN 85635 257 8 (Carcanet New Press Ltd. Paperback £2·00)

C. H. Sisson's new collection, *Exactions*, is a remorseless but distinguished one. These payments forced from him by the gravity of experience are made in an undebased coinage; it weighs cold and hard. Sisson's mind is working on failures of meaning, and though our world may be a desert in which to find God, his concern is with the nature of sand, dry-heartedness, absence. *Au Clair De La Lune* echoes the probing negatives of Eliot's *The Hollow Men* and the doubtful quest of his *Journey of the Magi*:

This is the end of everything, of everything, of everything
This is the end of everything
On Christmas day in the morning.

The spiritual aridity is tempered by a dry wit. Eliot's camels may be sore-footed and refractory; Sisson

> . . . came through that territory
> With camels, at least I had the hump.

This curiously entertaining tone, using the occasional techniques of light verse and nonsense verse to deflect the deficiencies of a non-rational universe, is an agreeable relief, but though poems such as *Reason* and *The Zodiac* have a sprightly diablerie about them, the power of the collection lies in its sober sequences *The Pool* and *Burrington Combe*. These poems, where flesh and spirit crumble, have a dark timbre relieved by the ease of Sisson's cadences and the fresh selflessness of the images he draws from the natural landscape about him. *Burrington Combe*, particularly, has a sense of hover and displacement reminiscent of the moods of Edward Thomas. The poem is moving because image and thought blend to one complexion, and the purely abstract thinking is left behind. At its best Sisson's poetry is of night, age, declensions—assured in its lack of assurance. Night falls, a curtain on zero:

> And it does fall, it is falling now
> The light is less already, see how it goes
> Smaller, smaller, smaller, the circle of light;
> But the scent of the rose
>
> The scent of the wallflower, the night-scented stock
> The scent of thyme, never off my hands
> Except when rue chases it, or fennel, or sage
> —Whose hands?—

Simon Lowy's dancingly adroit and affirmative *Melusine & The Nigredo*. The poems are divided into alchemical sections: Sulphur, Salt and Mercury. These three commodities may have hermetical correspondences to soul, body and spirit; the poetic alchemist in this dazzling set of love poems is trying for some apotheosis from the uniting of male and female principles. For the general reader, whose knowledge is definitely of the lesser rather than the greater arcana, the alchemical terms form a stage-setting for a virtuoso juggling performance with language. Simon—'& Omnis is the anagram of my name'—Lowy is at home in a baroque world of conceits, emblems, and word-play. If Edith Sitwell had been a chess-playing Metaphysical poet some of her poems might have looked something like some of these. It is a small triumph to have the nerve and brio to fly in the face of so much of the flat fustian stuff which crowds our current anthologies: 'Find your voice and having found it sing!' Yes, and the quality of the song is enticing:

> Chanterelle she,
> Nonchalant he.
> The sky she trod beneath, he loved,
> Her foot: ten driven nails as snow,
> Her fingers: arched above the cruel tea,
> Her lips, her two-times eyes, twice brow.
> So we swim for recreation
> In each other's inundation.

PETER SCUPHAM

Opposite page:) *Flute Totems* by Bob Cobbing.

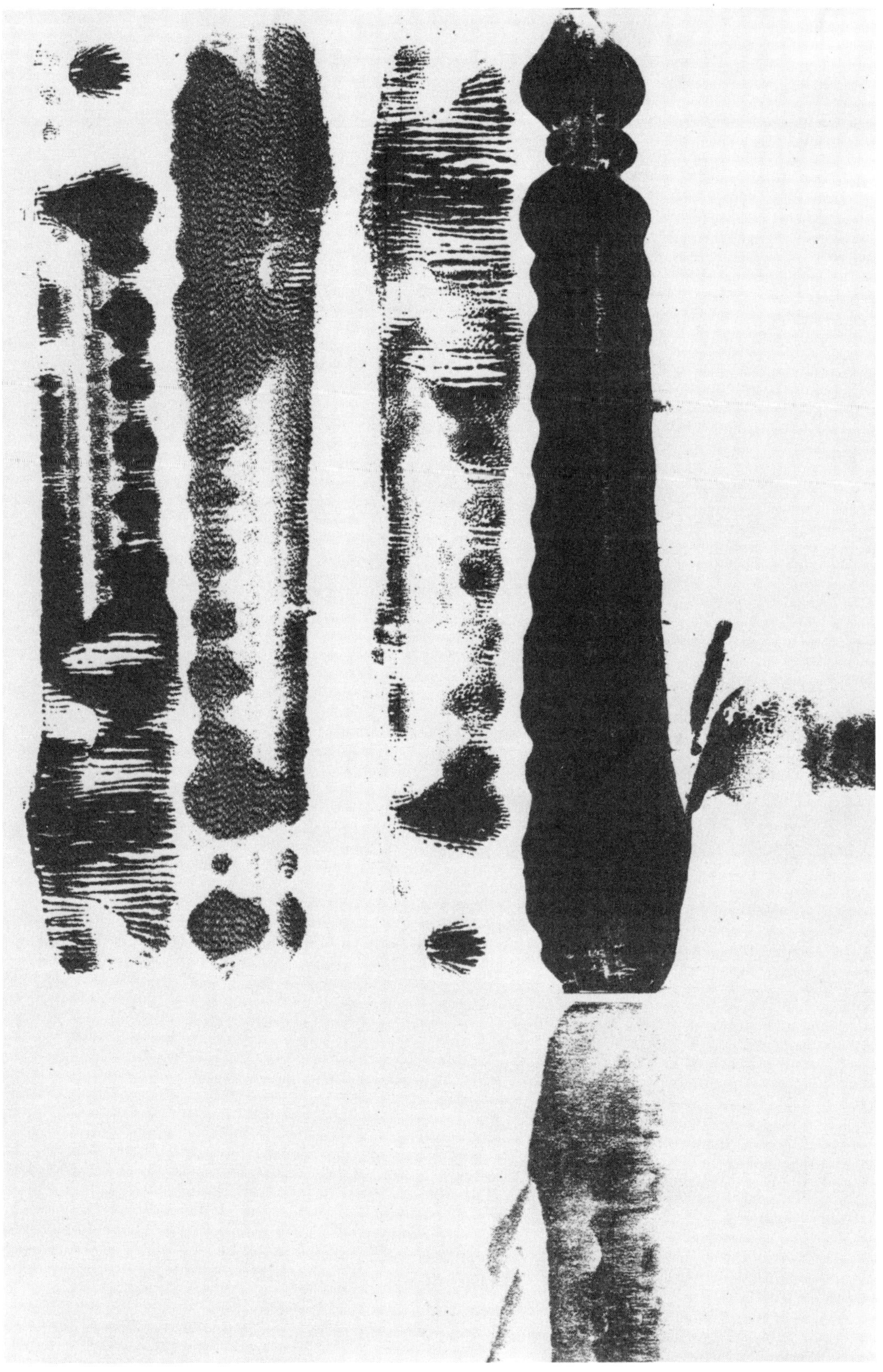

Henri Michaux

TELEGRAM FROM DAKAR

Evening, black,
car in the country,
baobab-trees,
Baobabs, Baobabs,
Baobab Plain.

Baobabs plenty baobabs
baobabs
nearby, distant, all round,
Baobabs, Baobabs.

Evening, black,
under low, pallid, shapeless clouds,
ragged, dirty,
shredded cloud chased hard
by an unfelt wind,
under clouds for mourning,
still as dead are the baobabs.

Curse!
A curse on HAM!
A curse on this continent!

Village
sleeping village
village gone

Out again on the open plain: Baobabs
Baobabs baobabs Baobabs
Africa prey to baobabs!

Feudal men of the Savannah. Old Scorpion-men.
Stubborn ruins. Outposts of the Savannah.
Morbid tom-toms from the Land of Misery.
Rituals of a fearful continent
Baobabs.

Village

Black men
Blacks so much blacker than tan
Open black faces swallowed by the night.
We talk to headless men
headless men answer in dialect
the night steals back their gestures.
Levelled faces, smooth moulded faces suspended
village of black faces
village of one moment
village gone

Baobab Baobab
    Eternal problem, planted there.
    Petrified—aggravated
    box-tree with heavy-boughs
    elephantine arms it cannot flex.

Oh great spaces
Oh dark distances brooded over by other
  Baobabs
    Baobabs, Baobabs, Baobabs
    Baobabs I shall never see
    stretching to infinity. Baobabs.

Sometimes, a bird will take off, very low,
    sluggishly, like a rag,
    A Moslem glued to the ground implores Allah
    No more Baobabs.

Oh sea never again as bitter
The port in the distance shows its little
    claws,
  (tiny harbour fiercely embraced).

No more
No more
No more Baobabs
baobabs
baobabs
maybe never more
baobabs
baobabs
baobabs.

Translated from the French by Geoff Thompson.

Robin Williamson

SONG OF MABON

(As Joseph Campbell has shown, the one hero of human myth has a thousand faces and a thousand names. The following piece is an excerpt from a work in progress which deals with this hero under one of his Celtic disguises—Mabon, the wild huntsman, stag-horned rider of the storm wind and the dark. It relates the progress of this mythic figure from midwinter to spring, and deals with the relationship of the poet to that lady in all women whose breasts are the hills of the world. A recording of the poem by the poet, who is one of the founding members of the Incredible String Band, is attached to the inside back cover of this issue.)

a telling to be told where journeys are broken
by fall of night or by first light of day
a secret to be spoken where turnings are taken
at spring's first flower or first shower of snow
a song to be whispered to ears that will listen
for love of the red rose, for love of the white rose

it is of the royal road by mayday and midwinter and summer's end
it is of the boundaries of the world and the other world
it is of the choice made when no choice is given
and of the weight of the horned mask on the face
by the gallows, the cradle, and the bridal feast
I have retraced the wild huntsman's way

a road avoided, overgrown, beset with thorns
a snaring way of dark and bitter verity
trod neither by saints of the earth nor the damned of heaven
a pure and crucial road or no road at all
a road of ghosts part beast part man part god
a cursed undutiful wandering that hurts my soul
stony, perverse, obscure
and beset with thorns

Thou frost white rose, Thou rose of fire
I have craved safe avenues and well-frequented love
some armament to raise against the cold
some grave, some mirror, not to be seen beyond
when first I could no longer
fail to see reflected in the water
simple and mad that light of the distant star
I entered in the spirit of the thing
cheerfully enough and long ago
I entered like a badger about his business
like a snake in love
like a man
carrying my bread and salt with all conviction
unsheathed, not scatheless
I have emerged

'red blood runs from the mouth of the white deer
the red-eared hounds are white as the snow is white'

'Lady, accept these words
I wear the huntsman's rags
I have pursued the darkness of my heart
into that place where all the colours of the world
are sacrificed to blindness
where the flame that warms the world's heart
is consumed in darkness'

'red blood runs from the mouth of the white deer
the red-eared hounds are white as the snow is white'

'Lady, accept this love
I have lost the huntsman's guile
following the footprints
of that which was lost beyond oblivion
I stumble on and on with what I have killed
striking my feet against law's sharpest stones
slurred and repetitive as a drunkard's lies'

'while the cock crows and spills in the cat grass
the moon must dream her cruel and tender dreams'

'cold cracks to the drone of lust and fear
outcasts in their stables clutch at straws
the untouchable retains its mystery in drowning
I sing the alchemy of the dead and the unborn
I sing the dark origins of future time'

'while the cock crows and spills in the cat grass
the moon must dream her cruel and tender dreams'

'Lady, accept this mask
my thought never strays from thee
I follow through the lost ways and the low
that which has passed beyond oblivion and death
there was a wheel, a silver wheel
a wheel sword-edged
a wheel or a year of time
a round tower of nine gates
a cage of bone
a ring, a broken key
a stone like glass
a tree where the white owls mourn
a well, an open eye
that weeps black tears

where true dreams die
a treachery hid in words and human blood
as seas flood at the beck of the white moon'

'red blood runs from the mouth of the white deer
the red-eared hounds are white as the snow is white'

'Lady, I am a figment, I am a blight, I am an ember
one mirror for all memory that steals what is true
a voice buried in my heart is crying
I am the pain of all the world
carry me with you'

'will you hear the singing of the cold mouth
fine, wily, words
fine, wily, words
fine, wily, words,
wine, wily, words . . .'

'alas and ochone'

'finding all faces of the dice are blank
I forge in the impression of my ritual war
truth against the world, truth against the world
no trust is given that is not the trust eternal'

'kiss—whisper
thorough—care
touch—deep
come—crying
the bone of a white hare
the bone of a grey sheep

the skull of a seabird
are lying white among the green grasses
milk white are these drops I sing'

'alas and ochone'

'the messenger springs in his feathers to the hills'

'awake you pale and ageing rhymer, toll the bells
and clash to the beakers of the brazen bells
the leaden bell tongues
for sword-clash and man-tongue fail away'

'Lady, as Thou in brightness shadowed be
perfect Thou my conception in women's eyes

I know for whom it is they rake the ashes of the fire
unburnt and unforsaking in the turning of the silver wheel
and taking nothing from the vale of no return
I have become the huntsman to unhood a cast of hawks
I have become the huntsman to call on the hounds
who but I shall wind the wild horn
and from the dark mystery pass again'

'hear thou the hoofbeats of the horse of Arion'

'maidens wash their faces in the dews of Caerleon'

'ruined halls are full of the smell of myrrh'

'young girls with arms outflung and flying hair
whirl dancing on the slopes of Caerleon'

'between the paps of Fife a spur of daylight breaks'

'I stand upon the black rock
I walk between the yellow and the gold
I listen at the earth for the echo of the music that is gone'

'and is it like the sea?'

'the sea I hear
always the sea
from whence the blood red sun swims up'

'though the wren die on the ivy bough
the road to may morning rises in the sea'

There is a dream within all dreams at rest
as calm is the place fair-beached between the sullen seas
where the singing birds heed neither night nor day
where the salmon's pool is shaded by the hazel leaves
between the trees the eagle and the ram
as language stands between the blood and air
and the figured wind must hush his hand of cold
and the summer stars scattered, are like flowers there

There is no jewel outstares that silver sheen
the snake of gold is twined about Her blossom chair
nor river harp to rhyme her gentled gaze
who in Her eyes all yearning and laughter bears
in love of Whom the thunder springs and falls
the morning star flings forth the shadowed day
and years must turn and old and young return
that the huntsman's song be tuned again to the green of may

John Cooper-Clarke

SALOME MALONY

I was walking down Oxford Road
Dressed in what they call the mode
I could hear 'em spinning all the smash hits
At the Mecca of the modern dance—The Ritz
Me feet fox-trotted and me shoulders did the shimmie
The bouncers on the door said 'gimmie gimmie gimmie'
I gave 'em the tickets, they gave me the shits
No healthy arguments in the Ritz
Standing by the cig machine who did I see
In lurex and terylene she hypnotized me
I asked her name and she said its
Salome Malony, Queen of The Ritz
Lacquered in a beehive, her barnett didn't budge
Wet-look lips, she smiled as sweet as fudge
She had a number on her back and sequins on her tits
The sartorial requirements for females at The Ritz
A man making like Fred Astaire complete with spats and tails
A Douglas Fairbanks moustache, dirty finger-nails
Whose snide innuendo was as subtle as the blitz
Waltzed off with Salome in his greasy little mits
Standing in the dandruff light trying to get pissed
Among the head lice, Old Spice, Brut and Body Mist
How can she be seen dead dancing with that dick
Her being Salome, el supremo of The Ritz
Tables flew, bottles broke, the bouncers shouted 'Lumber'
The dummy got too chummy in a Bing Crosby number
The glass globe dropped, cut the crowd to bits
Meanwhile, what about the queen of The Ritz
When the ambulances came she was lying on the deck
She fell off her stiletto heels and broke her fuckin' neck
The band threw down their instruments, the management threw fits
She's dead, she don't bring the business to The Ritz
The over-21's night said it was a shame
The dee-vor-cee club will never be the same
Joe Loss killed himself, Vic Sylvester quit
When the death dance drama did away with The Ritz
When the Last Waltz withered, the quick-step stopped
The ladies excuse me was permanently blocked
And Mecca made a living selling little bits
Of Salome Malony, in the wreckage of The Ritz

Tom Pickard

LETTER TO JOANNA

I

Warsaw/London Express

half awake
  from a rough
night's ride
  my neighbour (an old
Polish peasant)'s
  back hurts

he cuts pieces off
  an apple
which sizzles
  at the steel
assault

  his big hands
slice slivvers
  of skin
with a knife
  which is
a friend to him

his familiarity
  with the blade
is ancient

passing me the fruit
  he gestures
'to refresh the mouth'

on the edge of our seats
  we gaze at the land
with the confidence of dawn
  he mutters

thick mist
  through dark woods
your scent on my scarf

  we roll slowly
over another border

II

Berlin

outside every
  unlocked door
soldiers stand
  legs spread
thumbs tucked in
  gun-belt buckles

another leads
  an unmuzzled
German wolf-hound
  pulling on it's chain
as they search above
  below
and through the belly
  of our train

Ian MacCallum

COWBOY DIARY

Three-quarter moon rises at ten o'clock
into a star-decked sky,
I ride down to the nearby saloon
to hear the old songs and cry,
a few beers, a few dances, a few kisses
stolen from a tall dark stranger, then sigh
at closin' time, ride home in the moon shadows
and find a drunken Navajo on my doorstep, the very same guy
who stole my radio last year, but I don't fly
off the handle, just give him some coffee
and show him a bed, dive into my own and die
after hidin' the bullets and money under the floorboards—
Tomorrow (that's his name, he says), after huevos and frijoles, when the sun's risin' high,
I'll take him down the road apiece, he says he has another friend,
tell him I wish I could do more for him, it's the same old lie,
come home, feed and water the stock, fix that broken stretch of fence,
and see if there are enough apples left for a Sunday pie.

Matthew Sweeney

A SHOT IN THE DARK

(in memory Peter Sellers)

The joker is gone from the pack.
Today your friends, family
& a few of your wives gathered
to walk you away.
Now they return to the future
where cars will stall as always,
queues will form in public urinals,
and today some will talk of you.
The joker is gone, they'll say—
and you were that: Insurgent
of a brakeless laughter,
the clear grin the other side of scorn.
Goodbye is a shot in the dark
that ricochets into space,
is a shadow's mouth moving.
Forger of accents,
your old French raincoat walks alone.

Theater of All Possibilities and William Burroughs

DECONSTRUCTION OF THE COUNTDOWN

A Space Age Mythology

In *Deconstruction of the Countdown*, the Theater of All Possibilities presents their dramatic adaptation of William Burrough's work as a space age mythology. The scenes and extracts chosen here are those which best express the incisive and poetic quality of the script while maintaining the continuity of the play. A video tape presentation of the entire play has been released by Poetry London and Cine Ciao.

Deconstruction explores Burrough's proposition that conditioned scenarios of Word and Image association can be cut up to free perception from habitual patterns and thus enable a more creative and appropriate response to human life—to 'deconstruct the countdown' to world explosion.

'Cut-ups, which were developed by Brion Gysin, (are) simply applying techniques that were already pretty old hat in painting—the montage technique—which is much closer to the actual facts of perception than so-called representational painting. Suppose you walk around the block and you come back and put what you have seen down on the canvas . . . well, you've seen a jumble of fragments, you've seen half a street-sign cut by a car, and so on . . . To my way of thinking, Art, the function of Art—of any creative thinking, scientific thinking—is to make us aware of what we know and don't know that we know. People knew the Earth was round, they believed it was flat. When Cezanne's canvases were first exhibited people did not see that these were objects seen in a certain light from a certain angle. And they were so infuriated they attacked the canvases with umbrellas in some cases. But now any child can look at a Cezanne and say: That's a pear . . . or a fish. This expansion of consciousness, once it becomes established, then becomes a permanent part of consciousness. Like Joyce made people aware of their own stream of consciousness and he was considered unintelligible, but he wouldn't be—at least certainly *Ulysses* would not be—considered a difficult or unintelligible book at the present time.'

William S. Burroughs
The Planet Earth Conference
Institute of Ecotechnics
Aix-en-Provence, France. 1980

SCENE 1

THE MEET CAFÉ SIGN-UP

[*The Composite City. Senders, Divisionists, Liquefactionists, Latah. The Waiter is a replica of Napoleon. Singer.* URANIAN WILLY, THE HEAVY METAL KID, *disguised as an American Tourist, enters.*]

SINGER

Meet Café Song
1 2 3 4 5 6 . . . Countdown!
It ain't the same old Town.
No time for diamond rings and gowns,
Hardly time to go down
Waitin' for the Blow-up
Nothing's gonna slow up
Nobody's gonna throw up
No help is gonna show up
All systems on Go
Oh oh oh
Would anybody do it?
You bet your sweet life they would.
Would anybody do it?
You bet your sweet life they would.
Do what? Do what? Do what?
Blow the whole thing up.
Would anybody really do it?
Yeah——the Nova Mob!

WILLY

[*nasally*] Napoleon! Napoleon! Café! [*He monitors the café.* HASSAN-I-SABBAH *enters, sits down at* WILLY'*s table.*] My old enemy, Hassan-i-Sabbah!

HASSAN

Nova Police, Tangier. Your application for Biologic transfer off of junk is going through the appropriate channels. Right now our agents are searching your room.

WILLY

Yeah, Willy the Fink. I squealed. But why not? I saw I was just another mark like the others on this Dead Whistle Stop. Except they considered me no longer reliable. I had gone broke, so they had me down for Total Disposal in the Ovens.

HASSAN
Now you wish to work with us?
WILLY
What's the scene?
HASSAN
The Nova Police's work on the planet's addiction to being ruled by criminals can be compared to apomorphine's work on junk addicts, a regulator that need not continue after its work is done. Any man doing a job works to make himself obsolete. That should go double for police.
WILLY
I'm interested. I'm interested.
HASSAN
The Crab Nebula Supernova observed by the Chinese in 1054 A.D. was an exploding star. A band of Nova Criminals set off the bomb, they themselves escaping to this solar system with the objective of blowing this one up after they exploited it for all it's worth. Before they blow up a solar system they pick out a spot as many light-years away as possible. Ever notice we don't have as much time as people had say a hundred years ago? Take your clothes to the laundry, pick up your mail at American Express and the day's gone—they are short-timing us as many light-years away as possible. Ever notice something sucking all the flavour out of food, the pleasure out of sex, the colour out of the cities? Precisely the low pressure area that leads to Nova. Then the Mob moves across the wounded galaxy always ahead of the Nova Heat—That is, they did—the earth happens to be our set—and we intend to catch them with our antibiotic handcuffs.
WILLY
So why did I go along with blowing up the planet? Now you see it now you don't. Yeah, man, flesh and junk and charge stacked up—bank vaults full of it—Then after Nova Day we leave the bloody apes behind and on our way rejoicing, right?
HASSAN
Then you defected from the Nova Mob, opted for our Plan D—Total Exposure. Wise up all the marks everywhere. You were number one Sucker, you know the ins-and-outs. Show them the rigged wheel of Life-Time-Fortune. Storm the Reality Studio. Retake the Universe.
WILLY
How do you actually make an arrest? These guys aren't obvious.
HASSAN
Not only not obvious, friend Willy, but Nova Criminals are not even 3-dimensional organisms, though they are quite definite beings. They need to operate 3-dimensional human agents to achieve existential results. The point at which the criminal controller intersects a 3-dimensional human agent we call a 'co-ordinate point' and the little giveaway that carries over from one human host to another allowing us to detect the identity of the criminal controller is *habit*. To work with us you must obtain names and co-ordinate points. As dedicated men, we would sacrifice you or any other agent to stop the Nova Mob from exploding the Solar System.

SCENE 2

WILLY FINKS ON THE NOVA CONSPIRACY

[*London apartment.* WILLY. HASSAN *with microphone, tape recorder.*]
HASSAN
All right, Willy, sing. This time it's for the tapes and that'll be it for you with the Mob.
WILLY
I awoke from the Sickness at the age of forty-five. Most survivors do not remember the delirium exactly. I apparently took detailed notes on sickness and delirium: Naked Lunch—a frozen moment when everyone sees what is on the end of every fork.
I used Junk in many forms—morphine, heroin, delaudid, eukodol—I smoked junk, ate junk, sniffed it, snuffed it, piffed it, puffed it, injected it, shoved it up my ass.
HASSAN
And the result . . .?
WILLY
Addiction.
HASSAN
So you're an anti-drug crusader.
WILLY
I do not refer to keif, marijuana or any preparation of hashish, mescaline, Bannisteria Caapi, LSD, Sacred Mushrooms or any other drug of the hallucinogen group. They are considered sacred by those who use them, they create Peyote Cults and Bannisteria Cults, Hashish Cults, and Mushroom Cults—'the Sacred Mushrooms of Mexico enable a man to see God'—but no one ever suggested that junk is sacred. There are no opium cults. Opium is profane and quantitative like money.
HASSAN
What do you mean, like money?

WILLY

Junk pyramids, one level eats the level below. It is no accident that junk higher-ups are always fat and the addict in the street is always thin. There are many junk pyramids feeding on peoples of the world and all built on basic principles of monopoly: 1. Never give anything away for nothing. 2. Always catch the buyer hungry and always make him wait. 3. Always take everything back if you possibly can. The Pusher always gets it all back. The addict needs more and more junk to maintain a human form . . . buy off the Monkey.

HASSAN

Then why does anyone ever buy?

WILLY

No sales talk necessary. The client will crawl through a sewer to beg to buy . . . The junk merchant does not sell his product to the consumer, he sells the consumer to his product. He does not improve and simplify his merchandise. He degrades and simplifies the consumer. He pays his staff in junk.

Junk yields the basic formula of the Nova virus: The Algebra of Need. The face of 'evil' is always the face of total need. Beyond a certain frequency need knows absolutely no limit or control. In the words of total need: 'Wouldn't you?' Yes you would.

A word to the wise guys.

SCENE 3 finds Willy sleeping, to be awoken by a Venusian Boy-Girl who tries to lure him into cooperation. He resists the 'insane urge to kill a 3-D organism' of which Hassan-I-Sabbah had warned him. The Venusian Boy-Girl turns rigid. Willy dials his unit watch radio, reports the 'host empty', and warns of the Nova criminal's transfer to other hosts: 'a woman, probably Italian. Pick up in a villa outside Florence. Also a brother operating in the same area as a banker.'

In SCENE 4, Willy interrogates Winkhorst, the chemist, on his experiments with altering hallucinogen drugs to effect the work of the Nova criminals by producing the 'heat syndrome'. Willy asks Winkhorst whether the same technique could be used with apomorphine to defuse the build-up to Nova Explosion. Winkhorst attempts to persuade Willy that the Nova Explosion is inevitable and to accept an offer of evacuation in return for sending back a report that there is no evidence of Nova activity on planet Earth. Willy declines the offer: 'What you are offering me is a precarious aqualung existence in somebody else's stale movie . . .'

SCENE 5

BREAKOUT AT THE RECONDITIONING CENTRE

[HASSAN *and* WILLY *in front of Reconditioning Centre, Lazarus Pharmaceutical Division.*]

HASSAN

They distracted you with a war film and gave false information as usual. You are inexperienced, of course. Now come along and we will get the real facts. [*Knocks at the door of R.C.* WINKHORST *answers.*] And now, Mr. Winkhorst, let's have the real story.

WINKHORST

You dumb hicks.

HASSAN

The information and quickly. We have no time to waste with such as you.

WINKHORST

All right—we'll talk. The cyclotron processes image—smaller and smaller, more and more images in less space pounded down under the cyclotron to crystal image meal. Image of both of us as good as he used to be, old showmen packing our ermines.

HASSAN

Enough of the show—continue.

WINKHORST

Sure, sure, but you see now why we had to laugh watching that dumb rube playing around with photo-montage. Like charging a regiment with a defective slingshot.

HASSAN

For the last time—continue with your statement.

WINKHORST [*singing*]

You hoped to get high
We cut it with speed
You dreamed to fly
We crashed you to bleed

You tried for metanoia
We gave you paranoia
You went out on your larks
We shot you down with narcs
Surrounded you in parks
And showed you—you are marks!

HASSAN
This, Willy, is a death dwarf—as you can see, manipulated by remote control—compliments of Mr. and Mrs. D.

WINKHORST
Images—millions of images—that's what I eat. Ever try kicking that habit with apomorphine? Now I got all the images of sex acts and torture ever took place anywhere and I can just blast it out and control you gooks right down to the molecule. [*He rolls his eyes.*] My Power's coming—my Power's coming, my Power's coming! I got millions and millions of images of Me, Me, Mee . . . [*To* WILLY.] You hick—you rat—called the fuzz on me—all right—I'm finished but you're still a lousy fink.

HASSAN
Address your remarks to me.

WINKHORST
You hick sheriffs! You'll never get the apomorphine formulae in time—Never! Never! Never! Human dogs! [*He collapses, sobbing. Barks ferociously*] Don't mind if I have another shot, do you? Lemme havva shot and I'll tell you something innaresting.

HASSAN
Good sir, to the purpose.

WINKHORST
Shit—that's what my human dogs eat—Beauty, Poetry, Space—What good is all that to me? If I don't get the image fix I'm in the ovens. All the pain and hate images come back. You understand that you dumb hicks?

HASSAN
Don't you think, Mr. D., it is in your interest to facilitate our work with the apomorphine formula?

WINKHORST
It wouldn't touch me—not with the habit I got.

HASSAN
How do you know? Have you tried?

WINKHORST
Of course not—If I allowed anyone to develop the formulae he would be out you understand? And it only takes one out to kick over my hypo tray.

HASSAN
After all you don't have much choice, Mr. D.

WINKHORST
I still mushroom the planet wide open for jollies. Come closer and see my pictures. I got screams—burning heavens, idiot—flesh the room in pink carnival! [WILLY *turns away, vomiting.*]

HASSAN
Police work is not pleasant on any level. [WINKHORST *on floor, eyes vacant, slobbering, whimpering like dog.*] And the apomorphine formula, Mr. D.?

WINKHORST
Apomorphine is no word and no image. Word begets image and image is virus!

[DR. BENWAY *enters with 2 attendants.*]

BENWAY
Get this fucking Irreversible Damage outta here. Bad for the tourist business. [*To* HASSAN *and* WILLY.] Gentlemen, welcome to the Reconditioning Centre.

ATTENDANT
What should we do with him?

BENWAY
How the fuck should I know? I'm a scientist. A pure scientist. Just get him outta here. I don't hafta look at him is all. He constitutes an albatross.

WINKHORST [*desperately—to* HASSAN *and* WILLY.]
I am at your disposal! Technical sergeant, I can work for anybody! Just gimme a shot!

ATTENDANT [*lets out a hog call.*]
Soo-eee! Soo-eee!

[WINKHORST *rushes up grunting and squealing; attendant herds him out.*]

BENWAY
Wise guy. No respect for human dignity. Sorry for the annoyance. Gentlemen, your visit flatters us. And since you are now headed for the Lobotomy Centre, I will tell you what Winkhorst was garbling. [*Attendent smiles benignly at* WILLY *and* HASSAN.]
Gentlemen, it was first suggested that we take our own image and examine how it could be made portable.

We found that simple binary coding systems were enough to contain the entire image. They required a large amount of storage space until it was found that the binary information could be written at the molecular level and our entire image concentrated in a code within a grain of sand.

WILLY

You penetrated the genetic code! Brilliant! [*Sound of dogs barking.*]

BENWAY

We found this image material is not dead matter, but exhibits the same life cycle as the virus. This virus released upon the world would infect the entire population and turn them into our replicas, but it was not safe to release the virus until we could be sure that the last groups to go replica would not notice. The molecule which we created permutates existing material, in short, churns out a variety of facts at the information level sufficient to keep so-called scientists busy forever exploring the 'richness of human nature' and 'our creative culture'.

HASSAN

So—our pain comes from damage to our image. Junk is concentrated image, and this accounts for its pain killing action! [*Electronic timer on his watch bleeps. Telephone rings.* BENWAY *answers it.*]

BENWAY

What's that? Monstrous! Fantastic! Carry on and stand by. Operation helicopter is indicated. [*To* WILLY *and* HASSAN] It seems the electronic brain went berserk playing 6-dimensional chess with the Technician and released every subject in the Reconditioning Centre! [*Splits*].

HASSAN

We nearly got caught ourselves this time. Fortunately one of our agents screwed up the Computer's functioning right on schedule. Now we must storm the Reality Studio while Benway's occupied and cut up the Image!

SCENE 6

STORMING THE REALITY STUDIO

[*Inner Sanctum of the Reality Studio. The Board of Directors in tuxedos, red underwear, cigars.* DR. BENWAY *presides.*]

DIRECTOR ONE [*to* BENWAY]

Why do you keep those trains going?

BENWAY

I maintain my railroads for the train whistles at lonely sidings, the smell of worn leather, steam, soot, hot iron and good cigar smoke, for the glass-covered stations and the red-brick station hotels.

DIRECTOR TWO

What do you want for dinner, boss?

BENWAY

I want a dinner of fresh hog's liver, fried squirrel, wild asparagrass, turnip greens, hominy grits, corn on the cob and blackberries. The hog must be an Ozark razorback fed on acorns, peanuts, mulberries and Missouri apples. My hog must be kept under discreet observation round the clock to insure that it does not eat anything unclean like bullshit, baby rabbits or dead frogs, the surveillance being unobtrusive so as not to render the animal self-conscious.

DIRECTOR TWO

When do you want this by, boss? A year from now?

BENWAY

Next Sunday at the latest.

DIRECTOR TWO

But boss how in the hell . . .?

BENWAY

Go to Hell if need be but find me such a hog.

DIRECTOR TWO

Yes boss.

BENWAY

Once found he must be brought here. As you know hog's liver that has been on ice for even a few hours is quite unfit to eat. The hog must be butchered in my kitchens and the twitching liver conveyed immediately to the skillet to be cooked in the bacon grease of another such hog.

DIRECTOR TWO

Well sure boss . . . We could crate the hog up and jet it out here.

BENWAY

Are you mad? My hog would be terrorized and this would surely have an adverse effect on its liver.

DIRECTOR TWO

Well boss we could take over an ocean liner, fix it up like an Ozark range and . . .

BENWAY

Are you trying to poison me? The hog would become seasick and I would lose my dinner. Obviously the hog must be gently wafted here on a raft slung between two giant zeppelins, a raft lifted bodily from the Ozark Mountains. My squirrels, blackberries and wild asparagrass will of course accompany the hog and send a farm boy with it—a thin boy with freckles. He will tend my hog during the trip. He will shoot and dress my squirrels. Then he will make himself useful in other ways.

DIRECTOR TWO

Boss, the hog is here.

[WILD BOYS *skate by, throwing dead leaves on* THE BOARD.]

DIRECTOR ONE

Boss, the wild boys is here!

HASSAN

[*Enters, with* WILLY] Listen to my last words anywhere. Listen to my last words any world. Listen all you boards, syndicates and governments of the earth, and you powers behind what filth deals consummated in what lavatory to take what is not yours—To sell the ground from unborn feet forever.

THE BOARD

Don't let them see us. Don't tell them what we are doing. For God's sake don't let that Coca-Cola thing out—Not the Cancer Deal with the Venusians—Not the Green Deal—Don't show them that—Not the Orgasm Death—Not the Ovens—

HASSAN

Listen: I call you all. Show your cards all players. Pay it all pay it all pay it *all* back. Play it all pay it all play it *all* back. For all to see. In Times Square. In Piccadilly.

DIRECTOR ONE

Premature. Premature. Give us a little more time.

HASSAN

Time for what? More lies? Premature? Premature for who? I say to all these words are not premature. These words may be too late. Minutes to go. Minutes to foe goal.

THE BOARD

Top Secret—Classified—For The Board—The Elite—The Initiates—

HASSAN

Are these the words of the all-powerful boards and syndicates of the earth? These are the words of liars cowards collaborators traitors. Liars who want time for more lies. Cowards who can not face your 'dogs' your 'gooks' your 'errand boys' your 'human animals' with the truth. Collaborators with Insect People with Vegetable People. With any people anywhere who offer you a body forever. To shit forever. For this you have sold out your sons. Sold the ground from unborn feet forever. Traitors to all souls everywhere. You want the name of Hassan-i-Sabbah on your filth deeds to sell out the unborn?

What scared you all into time? Into body? Into shit? I will tell you: '*the word*'. Alien Word '*the*'. '*The*' *word* of Alien Enemy imprisons '*thee*' in Time. In Body. In Shit. Prisoner, come out. The great skies are open. I Hassan-i-Sabbah rub out the word forever. If you I cancel all your words forever. And the words of Hassan-i-Sabbah also cancel.

BENWAY

Don't listen to Hassan-i-Sabbah. He wants to take your body and all pleasures of the body away from you. Listen to us. We are serving The Garden of Delights Immortality Cosmic Consciousness The Best Ever in Drug Kicks. And love love love in slop buckets. How does that sound to you boys? Better than Hassan-i-Sabbah and his cold windy bodiless rock? Right?

WILLY

Bring together state of news—Inquire onward from state to door—Who monopolized Immortality? Who monopolized Cosmic Consciousness? Who monopolized Love Sex and Dream? Who took from you what is yours? Now they will give it all back? Did they ever give any more than they had to give? Did they not always take back what they gave when possible and it always was? Listen! Their Garden of Delights is a terminal sewer. These are conditions of total emergency. I order total resistance directed against this conspiracy to pay off peoples of the earth in ersatz bullshit. I order total resistance directed against the Nova Conspiracy and all those engaged in it.

Minutes to go. Souls rotten from their orgasm drugs, flesh shuddering from their Nova ovens, prisoners of the earth to come out. With your help we can occupy the Reality Studio and retake their universe of Fear Death and Monopoly.

HASSAN

[*Confronting* WILLY] I would like to sound a word of warning—To speak is to lie—to live is to collaborate. There are degrees of lying collaboration and cowardice, that is, to say degrees of intoxication. It is precisely a question of regulation. The enemy is not man is not woman. The enemy exists only where no life is and moves always to push life into extreme untenable positions. You can cut the enemy off your line by cutting up his image. [*Lights out on* THE BOARD]

The Reality Studio's now occupied, Gentlemen: Stay tuned into the News!

In SCENES 7–10, of which Scene 9 is printed here, 'the victors cut up the images':

SCENE 7 is a cut-up of Hollywood's Western-version 'Good Guy 'gainst the black black villains'. On a folkloric Mexican village street, magic, sex and true power (in the guise of an old crone, a queer, a punk and a weathered killer) prevail over 'law', 'order' and tourist imperialism.

In SCENE 8, the hierarchy-oligarchy of medicine, impersonated by DOC BENWAY and his faithful assistant VIOLET THE BABOON, virtually cut up the ailing patient, while triumphantly singing out the 'good news': 'Never forget our glorious simian heritage . . . Do as the baboons do—when attacked by a bigger baboon, always turn and present your sugar bum.'

In SCENE 10, the WILD BOYS overcome the vast army of technomen by invoking the suppressed emotional/ instinctive forces of their organisms.

SCENE 9

THE DEATH OF MRS. D

[MR. B., MRS. D., *and two* NARRATORS. NARRATORS *alternate lines.*]
In the beginning was the word.
The word was and is flesh:
The word was and is sound and image.
Sound travels at the rate of 1114 feet per second.
Image travels at the speed of light: 186,000 miles per second.
Mr. B, at point B′, and Mrs. D, at point D′, are 1114 feet apart.
Mrs D screams: ' . . . *flesh flesh flesh flesh you stinking heel . . .*'
(She hopes her contempt does not show unprotected margin.)
Mr. B is equipped with a telescopic-sighted camera and a tape recorder.
The camera and tape recorder are synchronized so that when Mr. B sights the beginning word on the lips of Mrs. D, he takes her picture and begins to record.
One second later, he hears and records her words.
When he hears her words, he has already taken her picture.
Mr. B has taken a picture of Mrs. D one second *before* she manifests herself to him in word.
Mr. B has split Mrs. D's word from her image.
Mrs. D might well bellow out some further pleasantries.
Mr. B, feeling he has heard enough already, provides himself with a rifle.
Mr. B mounts the rifle and the telescopic-sighted camera on a tripod.
The rifle has a muzzle velocity of 2228 feet per second.
When Mr. B sights the beginning word on the lips of Mrs. D he squeezes the trigger and takes her last picture.
Half a second later, the bullet hits her square in the mouth and explodes her back brain.
One second later, he hears and records her last words: *flesh flesh fl . . .*
Mrs. D has ceased to exist half a second *before* he hears and records her last words.
Expose negative.
Wipe tape.
Not knowing what is and is not knowing, Mr. B knew *not* Mrs. D.
Mr. B is now at a point in space, 186,000 miles from Earth at point B″.
Mrs. D is back on Earth at point D″.
Mr. B has the same basic equipment but has substituted an E and G Bradly laser gun emitting intense beams of coherent light at 186,000 miles per second, capable of piercing the hardest substance, even diamond . . . laser guns on the table, how dumb can you be?
Mrs. D has amplified her voice to accommodate the altered distance relationship.
At one second *after* 4:00 p.m., Mr. B sights the ugly word on Mrs. D's ugly mouth.

Now, since Mr. B is one light-second away from Mrs. D, and it takes one second for her image to reach point B″, Mr. B has, needless to say, provided himself with a more powerful telescope to take a picture of Mrs. D . . . not at one second after 4:00 p.m., of course, but at exactly 4:00 p.m., present Earth Time.

One second later, Bradley's laser slices through Mrs. D's big mouth and on my way rejoicing.

Mr. B has taken the last picture of Mrs. D (for Dead)

Mrs. D is always dead when Mr. B takes her death picture, a second later.

Mrs D existed only in her last image and her last words, which arrive, of course, some hours later . . . so shut off the recorder . . . expose the negative.

Mrs. D's word and image never existed.

SCENE 11

HASSAN-I-SABBAH OVERCOMES THE SUBLIMINAL KID'S COUNTERATTACK

[BENWAY, *the* SUBLIMINAL KID.]

BENWAY

Okay, Subliminal Kid, our cover's blown. You are the last chance to counterattack the Reality Studio. Hit them below the awareness belt!

SUBLIMINAL KID

Just watch me push their buttons! They'll be so horrified by the images they'd do anything rather than wake up!

BENWAY

Marvellous, marvellous. [*Splits*]

[*The* SUBLIMINAL KID *in a director's chair, watches film. Montage of images: eating a long hot dog/oil well flaming into sky/gun shooting bullets into target/hand thrusting money into quivering hand. Dancing figures: Coca-Cola bottle, dollar bill, flag, junk needle, policeman. One by one each film image freezes.* SUBLIMINAL KID *rages and falls in apoplectic fit punching buttons.* HASSAN *enters, turns off switch; figures halt. Stage is bathed in white light.*]

HASSAN

Nothing is true. Everything is permitted.
Boards, Syndicates, Governments of the earth—Pay.
Pay back the colour you stole.
Pay Red—Pay back the red you stole for your lying flags and your Coca-Cola signs. Pay that red back to penis and blood and sun.

Pay Blue—Pay back the blue you stole and bottled and doled out in eye droppers of junk—pay the blue you stole for your police uniforms. Pay that blue back to sea and sky and eyes of the earth.

Pay Green—Pay back the green you stole for your money—And you, Dead Hand Stretching the Vegetable People, pay back the green you stole for your Green Deal to sell out peoples of the earth and to get on board the first life boat in drag. Pay that green back to flowers and jungle, river and sky.

Boards, Syndicates, Governments of the earth—pay back your stolen colours. Pay colour back to Hassan-i-Sabbah.